GUMP'S

SINCE 1861

GUMP'S
SINCE 1861

A San Francisco Legend

CHRONICLE BOOKS · SAN FRANCISCO

A Sue Katz & Associates, Inc. Book
Art Direction and Design: Rogers Seidman Design Team
Editor: Gareth Esersky
Contributing Writers: Nan Birmingham; Gary Bukovnik; Gareth Esersky; William Goulet; Susan Kohl;
Diane Dorran Saeks; Janet Lynn Roseman, researcher and head writer.
Photos ©1990 John Clayton
Photo stylist: Liz Ross
Published in 1991 by Chronicle Books, San Francisco, California

Printed in Japan.

10 9 8 7 6 5 4 3 2 1

Chronicle Books
275 Fifth Street
San Francisco, California 94103

PERMISSIONS

Excerpts appearing on pages 32, 33, 43, 46, and 47 from *Gump's Treasure Trade* by Carol Green Wilson, ©1949, reprinted with permission, HarperCollins.
Introduction from the catalogue of "Nagasaki and Yokohama Prints from the Richard Gump Collection, 1981" on pages 129-130 reprinted with permission, the Asian Art Museum of San Francisco, Avery Brundage Collection.

PHOTO CREDITS

Color: All color photographs in this book were taken by John Clayton except those listed below:
Asian Art Museum of San Francisco, Avery Brundage Collection (pp. 58, 128, 129); Sharon Beals (p. 114); Bruce Forrester (p. 103); courtesy of Ginori (p. 86 left); courtesy of Gump's Advertising Department (pp. 61, 83 top, 87, 90, 91, 126, 127); The McGuire Furniture Company (pp. 78, 79, 80) Mimi McAllister, Salway Press (p. 116); Scotty Morris (pp. 120, 122); Edward Owen (p. 77); Riverside Church (p. 42); Troy Staten (pp. 112, 113, 115); courtesy of Wedgwood/Royal Doulton (p. 86 right); Wells Fargo Bank (p. 21).
Black and White: John O'Hara, The San Francisco Chronicle (p. 74); Skelton Photography (pp. 40 bottom, 47); Smithsonian Institution (pp. 12, 20 bottom); Society of California Pioneers (pp. 18-19).

Half Title: 250 Post Street, 1909: This is where the store reopened in 1909 after the earthquake and fire.
Title Spread: Late 17th and 18th Century snuff bottles.

ACKNOWLEDGEMENTS

Larry Banka, Sylvia Benvenuti, Gary Bukovnik, Rand Castile, Mr. Chan, James H. Clark, Kristina Colangelo, John Curran, Colleen Dillon, Jean Dolmans, J. Shelton Ellis, Jr., William Goulet, Clariece Graham, Suzanne Gump, Marilyn Gump, Michael R. Hawley, Helen Heninger, Robert Johnson, Marilu Klar, Mimi McAllister, John McGuire, Robert Mahoney, Sandra Nath, Jane Otto, Jim Roland, Clarence Shangraw, Ji Ing Soong, Michelene Stankus, Jim Stearns, Michael Terzian, Margaret Watson, Laurie Platt Winfrey, and all of the staff at Gump's, without whom this book would not have been possible.

C O N T E N T S

TEXTURE

TASTE

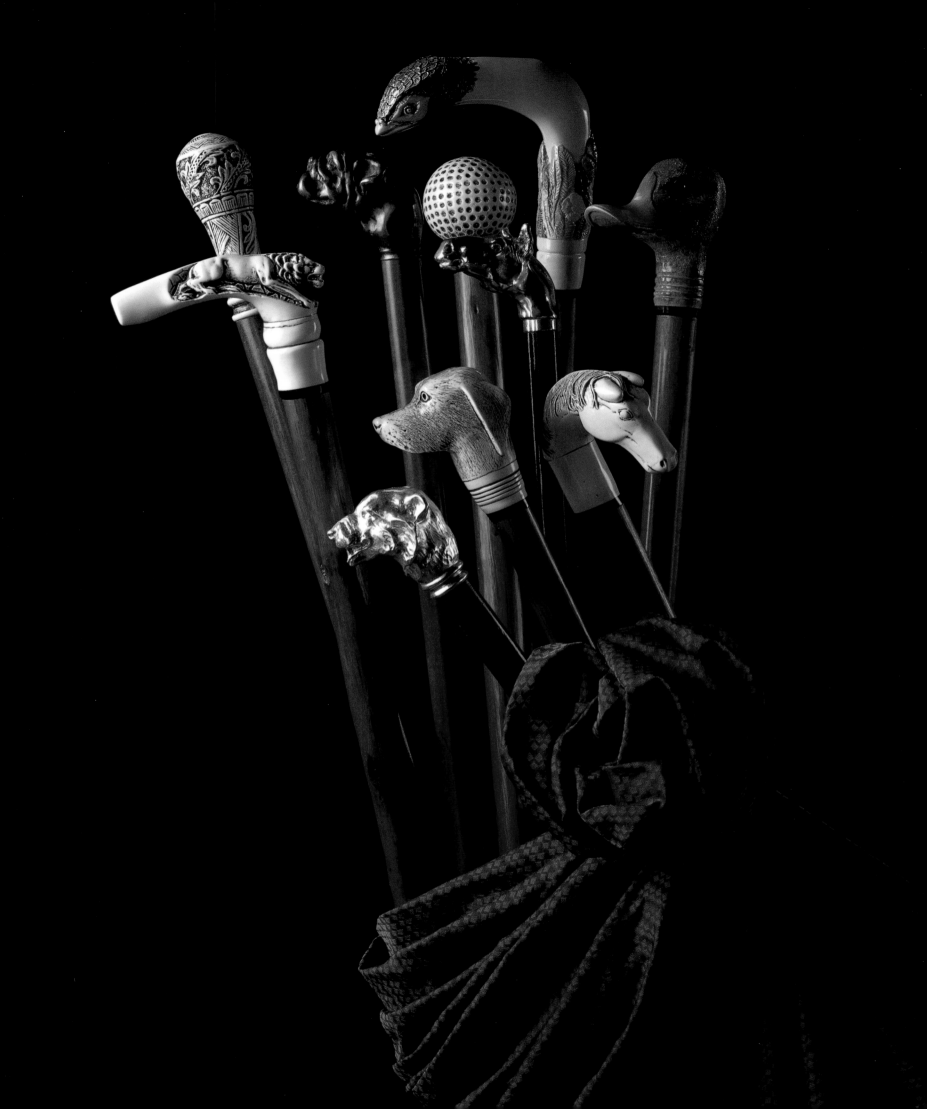

INTRODUCTION

Gump's Since 1861, A San Francisco Legend is a tribute to the quintessence of Gump's and an invitation to share in these pages the experience of being in the store. Gump's has become almost synonymous with the city of San Francisco, and, stalwart that it is, weathered at least two severe earthquakes, a major fire, and five relocations. This venerable retail institution has offered at least seven generations of San Franciscans and international visitors a guided tour of the world's treasures. In its early days, the store reflected the taste of the era and brought the Far East to the far West. It has displayed and purveyed a selection of goods as exceptional as the vision of its founders and the artisans and manufacturers who created them. Gump's Since 1861 is a San Francisco legend and much more than just the title of this book. It's the name knowledgeable shoppers and collectors, and not just San Franciscans, respect worldwide.

Love and respect for the store have been expressed by all those who have experienced it. The loyalty of staff—many of whom have been part of the store for over thirty years—is matched by the loyalty of patrons, customers, vendors, and artisans. The families in San Francisco who have toasted nuptials with a gift from Gump's for over a hundred years are matched by the families in the cities of Asia who have been representing Gump's for the same period of time. Closely woven into the tapestry of Gump's is the history of San Francisco and California. The Gump family's collection of woodblock prints displaying Japanese artists' impressions of the first years of western trade reflects an intimate and supportive relationship.

Gump's has always provided the elegant and the exotic and brought the world's treasures to America. Our buyers found beautiful objects and made them available to a large audience. They found the rare and unusual and made them an integral part of life. Our designers captured the past in contemporary application for ourselves and our environment. Gump's will proceed, designing and using an accessible path from culture to culture and from the past to the future. We will share Gump's treasures with a larger audience not only in America but throughout the world. We shall continue to create and provide wonderful things exclusively by Gump's. We count on celebrating our ongoing love affair with the world's most favorite city— San Francisco.

The opportunity to lead a venerable retail establishment with the status of a loved institution is not assumed lightly. However clear the vision for the future, there is always the risk of collision with images, memories and fond dreams of the past. Exploring and undertaking a new course for Gump's has revealed the richness of the past to be an important source for our future. Gump's is in the process of reinventing itself using the best of the past with the best that the future holds for our increasingly intimate world.

KENNETH WATSON
Chairman and Chief Executive Officer

WALKING STICKS HAVE BEEN THE FAVORED GEAR OF GENTLEMEN SINCE THE TIMES OF ANCIENT EGYPT. IT IS RECORDED THAT PERSIAN ROYALTY CARRIED WALKING STICKS AS EARLY AS 333 B.C. MORE OF A SYMBOL THAN AN ACCESSORY, THE WALKING STICK OR CANE HAS BEEN USED THROUGHOUT CENTURIES TO DENOTE PROPRIETY AND SOPHISTICATION. THERE WAS A TIME WHEN A MAN OF QUALITY WOULD NEVER STROLL OUT OF HIS HOME WITHOUT THE PROPER ACCOUTREMENTS OF HAT, GLOVES, AND CANE. THESE WALKING STICKS OFFER A RETURN TO A STYLE WHICH BY AND LARGE HAS DISAPPEARED. CARRYING A CANE INVOKES IN ITS OWNER THE BOULEVARDIER, SWAGGERING PROUDLY IN A CITY THAT BECKONS ITS INHABITANTS TO SAUNTER ALONG GRAND STREETS.

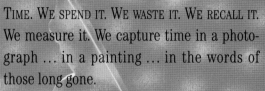

TIME

TIME. WE SPEND IT. WE WASTE IT. WE RECALL IT. We measure it. We capture time in a photograph ... in a painting ... in the words of those long gone.

Passing time gives us distance, softens the edges of life's trials and tribulations, and creates romance and mystery. At Gump's, the past becomes history, fable, and myth. Past times live in a tapestry of a scene from long ago, a collection of snuff bottles, a porcelain pattern, a silver epergne, a Japanese screen. Past times exist, too, in the family stories that share San Francisco's history and the beginning of an appreciation for the wonders of the Orient.

Present time reveals itself urgently and immediately in the tactile quality of contemporary craft. Present time has reduced distance, and the exotic becomes lovingly familiar. At Gump's, the future's plans and preparation are underway. Major occasions are marked, tomorrow's art treasures are displayed today, celebrations take shape. Gump's shares the legacy that links the past to the future.

THE LEGEND IS BORN

Gump's? It is a very *special* specialty store. It's *very* San Francisco. There are now Gump's stores in Houston and Beverly Hills, but roots were planted at the Golden Gate over 130 years ago. Gump's soul is as San Francisco as orange bridges and cable cars.

Solomon Gump, aged seventeen, arrived in New York in 1850, two years after James Marshall's housekeeper boiled a nugget from Sutter's Mill in a lye mixture to see if it was precious metal. Gold Fever broke out around the world. As a result of that primitive California alchemy, the Gold Rush was on—the greatest migration America has ever known.

Gump was thirty years old before he caught the disease and headed west, not for gold in the hills but to work in the San Francisco gold frame and mirror shop his brother-in-law, David Hausmann, opened in 1861. Giant gilt-framed mirrors behind the bars in Barbary Coast saloons were a bit of civility in the rip-roaring tent and shack town.

San Francisco was hardly more refined than mining camps such as Slumgullion or Jackass Gulch in those days. City streets were filled with mud, slop, horse droppings, and the flotsam and jetsam of humanity that washed up from the Pacific or swept down from the Sierras. They came from the Orient and Europe. South Americans fought and danced in Little Chili. Gangs from a penal colony in Australia were called "Sydney Ducks." During barroom brawls, Gump's mirrors were sitting ducks for flying bottles, bullets, and bodies.

The mirror and frame shop flourished. A year after his arrival Solomon bought out Hausmann, and sent for his wife and children and brother, Gustav. The store became "S. & G. Gump."

Behind the walls of the Spanish quarter there was a San Francisco that was seldom seen, where the old-line Californians, wealthy Spanish aristocrats, lived with dignity and grace. The new-rich kings of the Mother Lode bonanzas and later the railroad magnates were highly visible but longed for the culture and respect inherent in old money. These millionaires wanted all the trappings of wealth that money could buy. The nabobs built extravagant mansions on Nob Hill and Van Ness Avenue. They called on the brothers Gump to provide gilded cornices, gold leaf ceilings, whatever.

Eventually the Gumps were called upon to fill the frames that filled the grand salons. This necessitated trips

PREVIOUS SPREAD: THIS CARVED WOODEN BUDDHA IS BURMESE IN ORIGIN. THE RECLINING POSTURE SYMBOLIZES A BUDDHA WHO DWELLS IN THE REALM OF INFINITY AND SPACE, OF CONSCIOUSNESS AND NOTHINGNESS, FINALLY REACHING NIRVANA. BUDDHISTS BELIEVE THAT THERE IS MORE THAN ONE BUDDHA, EACH HAVING AN EARTHLY LIFE, BUT THERE IS NEVER MORE THAN ONE IN THE WORLD AT ONE TIME. BUDDHA COMES TO THE WORLD WHEN THERE IS A SPECIAL NEED FOR HIS PRESENCE.

ABOVE: DAGUERREOTYPE OF SAN FRANCISCO, C. 1850.

to Europe; they bought works for a new venture, the first art gallery in California. Gump's bought the sentimental landscapes and still lifes that dominated Victorian art. Solomon had an eye for voluptuous nudes on canvas—perfect replacements for broken mirrors. A life-sized Venus clad only in doves that hung over the bar in the Grand Hotel looked so real that patrons threw food to lure the birds from her provocative features. San Francisco was like that.

Years later Richard Gump spoke of his grandfather. "It was said he knew art. Truth is the nudes were paintings of his lady friend—a European actress. He didn't want her on display all over Europe." Gumps were like that.

Three generations of Gumps, San Francisco's leading purveyors of good taste, merchants of elegance who helped establish San Francisco as *the* American city with style of the highest order, kept tongues wagging with colorful liaisons, outlandish marriages, spicy divorces, and madcap antics. San Francisco delighted in their publicized exploits. Flamboyant, talented, often scandalous, Gumps were family. Gumps were reminders of the city's lusty past. Gumps were—like San Francisco—naughty with class.

As a result of his European philanderings Sol surfeited Mrs. Gump with presents. Rumor has it that one day she'd had enough. She sent the *chotchkas* off to the store with orders to sell them. Gump's was in the gift business.

Alfred Livingston Gump, Solomon's fourth son—called "Abe" for Sol's father, Abraham, and later "A. L.," by associates—was an impressionable child, in spite of or perhaps because of his poor eyesight. Abe was nearly blind. He adored going to Chinatown with the family's Chinese cook. He accompanied his father to mansions where he fingered rich fabrics and studied the best and worst in art and taste. The Chinese Room in Leland Stanford's Nob Hill palace was a favorite haunt. He admired the carved furniture, porcelains, and bronzes and began to nurture his love for Oriental art.

In 1906, shortly after A. L. inherited the store, the fire that followed the great earthquake destroyed much of San Francisco and all of Gump's. There was no money to rebuild until a "lady of the evening," Dodie Valencia, offered A. L. $17,000 for a painting he had at home. Gump's was back in business and Dodie's girls could get credit at Gump's ever after. As Gump's restocked after the disaster, A. L. felt the time had come to sell furnishings and objects from the Far East. Gump's opened a department of Oriental art.

Richard Gump, one of A. L.'s three lively offspring, became president of Gump's after the death of his father in 1947. A handsome man, Richard was multitalented. He worked as a designer for MGM and later designed everything for Gump's: jewelry, flatware, linens. He was a painter and composer. He wrote two best-sellers, *Jade: Stone of Heaven* and *Good Taste Costs No More.*

Under Richard Gump's aegis, the innovative Gump's Interior Design Department set new high standards for interior decor. Gump's Art Gallery gave fresh recognition to California artists—painters, graphic artists, printmakers, and ceramists. Richard personally guided Gump's staff members through American and European museums and galleries, teaching the finer points of art appreciation. His staff adored him for his humor and taste. Richard Gump's exhortation to San Francisco echoes loud and clear: "You can't afford an ugly thing at any price."

Like San Francisco, Gump's is old and young, traditional and modern, serious and fun, Occidental and Oriental. It's this enigmatic character that is the endearing charm of Gump's and San Francisco.

NAN BIRMINGHAM

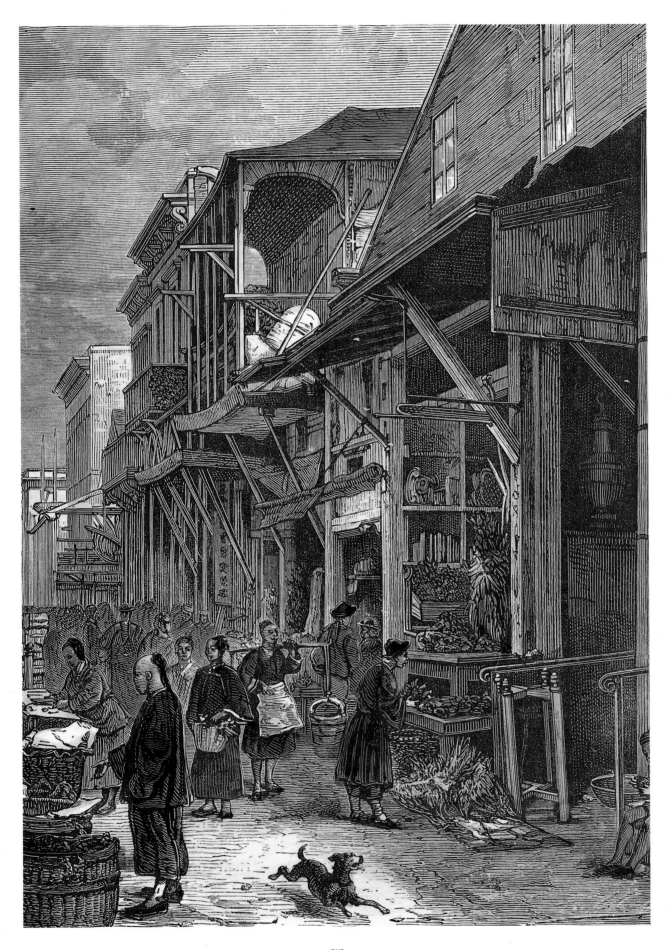

As a child, A. L. Gump often accompanied the family cook to grocery vendors and curio shops in old Chinatown. It was here he first encountered Oriental art and developed a passion that lasted a lifetime.

"GILD IT"

In the 1860s, the burgeoning aesthetic movement elevated good taste as an indicator of social status. Furniture and decorative items were considered "art," and A. L. Gump was quick to identify this trend and capitalize on it. By 1871, San Francisco was well supplied with millionaires, and a popular ritual was reading the "Mucho Dinero" column in the *Morning Call* to find out more about the fortunes of the self-made and very fortunate. Although the Oriental influence in home furnishings was becoming popular in Europe, decorating with gold was still very much in vogue in America. No one in San Francisco was bored with gold-plated fixtures, because as one wealthy patroness put it, "it doesn't ever need polishing." When a woman of rather large dimensions sailed into the store with a white enamelled toilet seat over her richly clad and bejewelled arm, she presented A. L. with a challenge. She demanded he "enlarge the opening of the seat four inches wider and ten inches longer," and as if that were not sufficient, she added, "and gild it. I always wanted to sit on gold." Her request was granted.

FROM SALOON TO SALON

There were many San Francisco taverns which were famous not only for their drinks and their air of hospitality but more because of the atmosphere created by their interesting and beautiful paintings. These gathering places of sociability passed from American life with the destruction of the great fire of 1906. They were more than mere saloons. Many were known the world over. They lasted long enough to launch many of the newly rich who frequented them on careers of art collecting. I could list a dozen famous collections whose beginnings can be traced to tastes acquired in the taverns of old San Francisco.

San Francisco was an art dealer's idea of heaven on earth in the late bonanza days. Early San Francisco typified the American yearnings for better things. The city in the 1890s was a cross-section of the American middle class. People had come to San Francisco from everywhere seeking fortunes and broader, richer living. They were not the poor, because the poor could not afford to come to California. They were not the rich, because the rich would not leave the luxuries and comforts of home to start anew in the raw, rough, new metropolis by the Golden Gate. Those who came did so to gratify the typical American wish for the short cut to affluence. Many of them realized their yearnings.

In the gay raucous city where everyone was making his fortune overnight, it was the custom of the leading citizens to gather around the bars at the cocktail hour of five o'clock. There the tycoons of the day met their cohorts, and the businessmen met their rivals and customers. The whole city knocked off work and gave itself over to sociability. The famous bars of the day were not ordinary saloons. They were grand palaces, as gay and attractive as their owners could make them.

ABRAHAM LIVINGSTON GUMP WITH FRANK J. TAYLOR
The Saturday Evening Post

SOLOMON AND WILLIE GUMP AT S. & G. GUMP.

"CALIFORNIA HERE I COME!": THE GOLD RUSH TO GUMP'S

When Solomon Gump arrived in Gold Rush San Francisco, the city was colorful and rowdy. It sprawled high and low and from hill to sea to accommodate the building boom that newly made fortunes created. Saloons and mansions alike were big business for enterprising merchants, for these edifices had to be constructed, furnished, and decorated. When the resourceful Solomon joined his brother-in-law David Hausmann in the birth of the little shop called Gump's in 1861, they became *the* providers of architectural and decorative ornamentation for the city by the Bay. Establishments in the citadel of sin and silver were flourishing wildly, and Gump's sold them polished wooden bars, sculpted marble ladies, and ornate mirrors, which, given the fractious nature of the activities in most saloons, they frequently and remuneratively replaced. They also manufactured the fancy picture frames, gilded cor-

nices, and mouldings for the homes of the Gold Rush citizens who had begun to settle down in a grand manner.

San Francisco in the 1880s was a paradise to art dealers and to those people who had gambled on a new life in the West and won. Fortunes were made in a hurry and spent the same way. A phrase used to express the mood of the era was "a mansion a minute," and Gump's seemed to be decorating them just about as fast. Nothing would do but imported paintings and objets d'art. Solomon and Gustav Gump shopped Europe from one end to another for works of art to complement these rapidly built and richly appointed showplaces. The objets d'art that Solomon found he purchased with his own collection in mind, but they were destined to become conversation pieces in the mansions of his treasure-hungry customers.

The store moved to a succession of locales over the years as Gump's expanded its merchandise, carried larger inventories, and enjoyed timely success. From 535 Clay Street to 119 Sansome Street in 1872, to Market Street in 1876 and Geary Street in 1892, the address changed, but the quality and distinction always remained. The economy couldn't have been better in the 1890s. These were great years in San Francisco—years of plenty, pomp and elegance, and prosperity for Gump's.

"I have seen purer liquors, better
segars [sic], finer tobacco, truer
guns and pistols, larger dirks and
bowie knives, and prettier
courtezans, here in San Francisco
than in any other place I have ever
visited; and it is my unbiased opin-
ion that California can and does
furnish the best bad things that are
obtainable in America."

HINTON R. HELPER
Land of Gold: Reality
vs. Fiction, 1855

"San Franciscans seem to harbor a mystical sense of mission—that they have been given the duty of introducing Good Form and The Right Thing to the wild and woolly West."

STEPHEN BIRMINGHAM
The Right People

The entrepreneurial Gump family epitomized this sense of mission. For over 130 years, Gump's has been the West Coast's premier purveyor of taste and style. Solomon Gump would be proud to know that the little shop modestly called "S. & G. Gump: Mirrors, Mouldings, and Paintings" would grow to become the store where the visitors were offered a taste of the world and its cultures and luxuries.

OPPOSITE PAGE, TOP: SAN FRANCISCO FROM YERBA BUENA ISLAND, C. 1870. AS THE CITY ROSE FROM ITS POST-GOLD RUSH VILLAGES OF TENTS AND MUD TO ONE OF BURGEONING PROSPERITY, THE MARKET FOR GUMP'S' GOODS WAS ESTABLISHED.

OPPOSITE PAGE, BOTTOM: SAN FRANCISCO HARBOR, 1852-53.

ABOVE: GOLD RUSH DAYS, TELEGRAPH HILL, 1849-50.

THEN AND NOW
S. & G. Gump Locations

❖ Founded in 1861 under the name of David Hausmann & Company, the first store was at 535-537 Clay Street.

❖ In 1864, Solomon bought out his brother-in-law David Hausmann.

❖ In 1872, the store was moved to 117-119 Sansome Street, with a factory established on Market Street between 7th and 8th Streets.

❖ In 1876, the store moved to 581-583 Market Street from the Sansome site.

❖ In 1892, a new locale of 113-115 Geary Street, near Union Square, was chosen.

❖ In 1906, the San Francisco earthquake and fire wiped out the Geary store.

❖ After the fire, Gump's set up at 1645 California Street, between Van Ness Avenue and Polk Street.

❖ By summer of 1909, Gump's was ensconced in its current Post Street store.

WHAT THEY SAID ABOUT GUMP'S

Everyone loves Gump's. Over the years, noted personalities have paused, at the guest books in the Jade Room or in print, to express their appreciation for such a remarkable institution.

"I spent a lovely afternoon at Gump's—that's all I spent."
JACK BENNY

"Gump's is the Metropolitan Museum with cash registers."
SALLY STANFORD

"I've always made a beeline for Gump's."
MARY MARTIN

"Visiting Gump's is like the climax of a long crescendo."
ARTHUR FIEDLER

"You will be built into the litany of culture in our West."
FRANK LLOYD WRIGHT

"It's beautiful and wonderful."
PATTY, MAXINE, AND LAVERNE ANDREWS

"I shall want to come back again and again."
BURGESS MEREDITH

"An inspiration."
EUGENE ORMANDY

"To the institution of Gump's…the fairyland of my childhood."
CAROL CHANNING

"To the only gentleman I'm afraid of, A real CHAMPION, Mr. Gump. With very good wishes for success."

JACK DEMPSEY

"Mr. Gump, I wish I knew my jokes as well as you know every piece of jade in your wonderful collection."

GRACIE ALLEN

"To Mr. Gump with sincere appreciation of the exquisite taste that led to the formation of one of the finest collections of art I have been fortunate enough to witness."

ARTIE SHAW

"A footsore and weary New Yorker, journeying afar in the Wildest West, found beauty at last and color and fancy and the most consummate art in the studios of A. L. Gump, collector and man of taste."

FRANK CROWNINSHIELD

"Still my favorite slice of San Francisco."

HERB CAEN

"The greatest store of its kind in the world."

THOMAS HOVING

AMONG THE GLITTERATI OF EACH GENERATION WHO ADDED THEIR NAMES TO THE BOOK ARE: GLORIA SWANSON, RAMON NAVARRO, DOUGLAS FAIRBANKS, MARY PICKFORD, CHARLES BOYER, JEAN HARLOW, ERROL FLYNN, NELSON EDDY, ALFRED HITCHCOCK, OTTO PREMINGER, CECIL B. DEMILLE, MARY ROBERTS RHINEHART, AMBROSE BIERCE, EDNA FERBER, EUGENE O'NEILL, CLAIRE BOOTH LUCE, ALEXANDER WOOLCOTT, FREDERICK LEOPOLD, PRINCE OF PRUSSIA, NELSON ROCKEFELLER, ELEANOR ROOSEVELT, HERBERT HOOVER, HELEN HAYES, SALLY RAND, MYRNA LOY, VINCENT PRICE, KATHERINE HEPBURN, BURGESS MEREDITH, ROSALIND RUSSELL, ALAN LADD, JUDY GARLAND, LAUREN BACALL, ROD STEIGER.

WHAT THEY WROTE ABOUT GUMP'S

In the early years of the firm Solomon and Gustav concerned themselves primarily with mirrors and mouldings, but increasingly they offered European and Oriental antiques. In 1906, after the earthquake and the fire, San Francisco business needed a boost. A catalogue extolling the city's virtues and venues was published to attract new business and tourism. This excerpt from the special edition of *The Monitor* was entitled "Meritorious Downtown Business Firms" and carried the subhead "How to Buy Antiques by S. and G. Gump."

S. & G. GUMP COMPANY

The craze for antiques has flooded the market with innumerable fakes until one hesitates before buying at all. Expert knowledge is essential and if the purchaser be deficient in this he must rely upon the word of men from whom he buys the article. Therefore, it follows that a man engaged in this business has to be thoroughly honest and reliable if he wishes to gain and keep the confidence of the people. The above named has a reputation for honesty which extends throughout the Diocese, where they have long enjoyed their liberal patronage. Gump's is one of the largest dealers in the city in European, Japanese, and Chinese fine arts, and has art pieces of every description.

The managers display taste and discrimination in the selection of their goods, the senior partner going every year to Europe and the East to choose the latest and best art productions in the world. The frames, mirrors, and mouldings are made of the choicest materials regardless of cost. The wooden mantels are used extensively in the ornamentation of many of the finest houses on the Coast, while the paintings and engravings sold by the firm beautify many of the finest halls and palaces.

The factory is a large four-story building located at 251 Jessie Street and is well-equipped with a supply of machinery embracing all the latest mechanical appliances that can in any manner facilitate manufacturing operations. The goods are made in different styles and of various sizes and give the best satisfaction to all patrons. The work is done by skilled journeymen under the direction of competent foremen. Nothing is allowed to leave the factory until carefully examined, the slightest defect being considered sufficient to condemn any article, however costly.

The trade territory of the firm embraces the Pacific Coast, Mexico, and Central America. The annual business is steadily increasing and now exceeds a quarter of a million dollars. The affairs of the various departments of this extensive business are conducted under the efficient system of management which comprehends every detail. Messrs. S. and G. Gump afford interesting examples to the rising generation of what may be achieved through untiring energy and a strict devotion to the interests of a business.

FOREIGN, OLD WORLD, AND ORIENTAL PIECES WERE AVAILABLE TO GUMP'S SHOPPERS AND COLLECTORS IN THE STORE'S EARLY YEARS. TODAY, VISITORS ALSO WILL FIND ANTIQUE VICTORIAN APPOINTMENTS AND ACCESSORIES.

FAMILY STORIES

Whether true or apocryphal, the Gump family stories share a common characteristic—a larger than life quality. It was the stature of Solomon, the theatrics of Mabel, the outrageous antics of Marcella, the extraordinary artistic sense of the near-blind A. L., the eccentricities of Robert, and the eclectic nature of Richard that made them stand out from the crowd. The Gumps enjoyed being noticed. They wanted to be trend-setters, to be first, or at least close to first, and in many cases they were. It was a trait that served them well as taste makers and marketers.

THE GUMP LADIES

MABEL BEATRICE LICHTENSTEIN GUMP   When beautiful Mabel Lichtenstein met Abraham Livingston Gump, it was only natural that there would be some "chemistry." A. L., the nearly blind art dealer, was absolutely smitten with the feisty and fiery young actress. When he first met her, he pronounced with his customary authority, "That is the girl I'm going to marry." In 1902 they did wed, and Mabel proved to be the perfect complement to A. L. Her trained speaking voice, which entertained so many theatregoers, gave him great pleasure, for as his sense of sight failed his sense of hearing became more and more sophisticated. Mabel spoke four languages and frequently read aloud to A. L., choosing classics and contemporary novels, often in the language of their origin. Even though they later separated, much to A. L.'s great regret, Mabel's love for him was very real. She told her son Richard that his father "had more sex appeal than any man I ever met."

Mabel acted in plays at The Little Theatre in San Francisco, but it was the great stages of Broadway and Europe that interested her. When she played Catherine the Great in "Big Kate" in Europe she was truly in her glory. She cut quite a figure, decked out in her own fine pearls, accompanied by a brace of Russian wolfhounds. Her flair for the dramatic included hiring young men to shower her with bouquets as she descended the stairways of some of the Continent's grandest hotels. She was offered an opportunity to extend her role of Catherine in a twenty-six-week run, but A. L. forbade it, according to their son Robert, thundering "No American gentleman would permit his wife on the professional stage!" But Mabel stayed on the stage despite A. L.'s protestations. Not only did she continue to act, she took the children, Richard, Robert, and Marcella, on tour with her when she played abroad, exposing them to high culture at a very early age.

An independent woman when it was not exactly in fashion, Mabel had a talent and a spark that ignited a whole generation of Gumps.

MABEL STARTS A TREND

In 1922, Mabel travelled to China with Robert. Shortly after they arrived, revolution broke out and headlines in the San Francisco papers reported that the Gumps had been lost in China in the midst of the unrest. Fortunately, the U. S. Marines rescued them. Mabel and Robert were urged to discontinue their travels in China, so they went to Japan, where they created an uproar of their own.

When Mabel appeared on the streets of Tokyo wearing a light green "haori" (overcoat) in a woven pattern of cherry blossoms, she and her handsome son attracted what they thought to be admiring glances. But when barefoot children followed them, laughing and pointing, Mabel was embarrassed and confused. Robert knew the children's fingers were pointing at his mother's coat, but he was nonplussed and at a loss to explain why. Years later, as Robert became more worldly-wise and more familiar with the traditions and customs of Japan, he was able to figure out what had happened. Apparently, Mabel had been wearing a coat intended for a geisha. Geishas were identified by the style of the haori, its woven symbols, and the cherry blossoms. Mabel was oblivious to the message her coat bore, but even if she had understood it, and the notion that the Japanese might have found such a gesture undignified, she might have flouted convention and worn her pale green haori just the same.

Mabel returned to San Francisco with seven of the beautiful, luxurious silk haori coats and several less expensive copies. When she modelled her new robes for her husband, A. L. knew he was on to something big. He ordered hundreds of the haoris and succeeded in creating a fashionable trend for the twenties.

FRANCES WIDNEY GUMP

Frances Widney Gump, Robert's first wife, had an impressive California lineage. Members of her one-time-pioneer family created a number of charitable foundations and institutions, including the University of Southern California, and held positions on the first Board of Regents for Stanford University. Robert, the Gump family philosopher and raconteur, captured her attentions and they were married in 1926; she happily exchanged her staid, conservative lifestyle for the exciting life of a Gump. A striking woman with topaz eyes and auburn hair, Frances also had a bit of the devil in her and a wonderful sense of humor. It was easy to see why Robert fell in love with her. She briefly designed window displays for Gump's, but her work as a floor model in the exclusive Fashion Room suited her best. Her lithe figure and sense of grace perfectly complemented the gorgeous Chinese robes she displayed. She later modelled for *Vogue* magazine.

Frances and Robert had two children, Suzanne and Marilyn. After eleven years of marriage the couple divorced. Robert left the family business and later shocked the entire family by marrying Sally Stanford, divorcing her after a brief two years. He left San Francisco and spent many years living in southern California and Mexico, writing. His book *You are the Rose, You are the Rock* was a cult classic during the flowering of San Francisco's Haight-Ashbury days.

FRANCES WIDNEY (MRS. ROBERT) GUMP, c. 1924, WHEN SHE MODELLED AT GUMP'S FASHION ROOM.

MARCELLA GUMP An attractive woman quite accustomed to getting her own way, Marcella inherited her mother Mabel's appearance, nonconformist attitudes, and love for the dramatic. She built for herself an exciting and out-of-the-ordinary life to match. Living in the South Seas on the island of Moorea with her husband of the time, Llewellyn Philips, she enjoyed many happy years.

Philips was well educated and had a degree from the Massachusetts Institute of Technology. He was an Amaru, one of the five ruling families of Tahitian royalty, and a descendant of King Pomare, the first king of Tahiti. Philips' father was related to the House of Prince Albert, the consort of Queen Victoria of England. His father's castle, Heath House, still exists today.

Although Marcella was not actively involved in the store's day-to-day operations, her tangential influence was apparent. Schooled in Europe, and supplied with all the opportunities Gump money could buy, Marcella spoke French, Italian, and Spanish fluently, and she developed a substantial amount of talent in the arts and exhibited her work. She travelled extensively as a young girl with her brothers and her mother while Mabel was performing abroad, and was exposed at a relatively early age to all aspects of Continental culture and custom. She surprised Mabel by taking it upon herself at the age of fourteen to have her portrait painted by a Parisian artist. This may seem like a fairly innocuous gesture—except for the fact that the painting was of Marcella in the nude!

MARILYN GUMP AND UNCLE RICHARD Marilyn and her Uncle Richard got along splendidly. Theirs was a relationship of mutual admiration, love, and lots of fun. They spent uproarious times together, frequently having what Richard called "theme evenings" during which they would converse in a particular accent or foreign language. Sometimes Richard would want to speak in Shakespearean iambic pentameter, while on other occasions the two would sing and play music together until the early hours of the morning, recording their entertainments in a series of improvisational tapes. Clearly, an evening with any of the Gump family could never be termed "ordinary."

SUZANNE GUMP AND THE BUDDHA In the early 1930s, when Suzanne Gump was a very small child, she accompanied her mother on visits to the store. Suzanne was fascinated with and a little bit afraid of the bronze Buddha that towered over the Silver Department on the first floor, before the Gump family donated it to the city and it was moved to Golden Gate Park. Barely able to reach its pedestal, Suzanne remembers one of the sales clerks giving her a long and intricate explanation of the symbolism and meaning of the grand Buddha. This brainy child listened intently and concluded that the reason everyone respected her grandfather A. L. was simply that he had "God" in his store.

THE BUDDHAS

"When he first appears, Buddha is already completely formed.. Thousands of statues of Buddha were fashioned with Buddha always assuming heroic proportions, resembling a warrior who has laid down his weapons to contemplate the carnage of the world. Huge chested, rather stiff and heavy, always seen frontally, wearing the gown of the Hellenistic philosopher with features ultimately deriving from a Hellenistic Apollo, with long pendulous earlobes and a third eye in the center of his forehead, he sometimes appears as a chakravarti, a world emperor, who orders the world by the massive power of his thought."

ROBERT PAYNE
The World of Art

A huge bronze Buddha named "Amazarashi-No-Hotoke" stands in the Japanese Tea Garden in Golden Gate Park. Translated, its name means "Buddha who sits throughout sunny and rainy weather without a shelter." A gift to the city of San Francisco from the Gump family in 1949, it was cast in Tajima Province on the island of Honshu for the Taioriji Temple in 1790 and bought by A. L. in 1928. It stood in the Post Street store for fifteen years until a rebuilding project consigned it to storage. When the wooden Buddha that formerly watched over the Tea Gardens was destroyed, the family donated Amazarashi-No-Hotoke in honor of A. L., Alfred, and Willie Gump.

The Chinese Buddha that appears on the cover of this book is splendidly gold-leafed. The largest of its kind extant outside a museum, this priceless million dollar statue stands guard inside Post Street to greet all visitors to Gump's. As the unofficial symbol of the store, and the only item that is not for sale, it bestows a serene and mysterious benediction upon all who enter.

A. L. AND THE IMPORTANCE OF LEARNING

A.L. Gump's fondness for literature was legion, his appreciation of the intellect admirable, and his quest for knowledge of the arts one of ongoing dedication. He passed this enthusiasm for learning and the arts from his generation of Gumps to the next and then to yet a third.

After the famed Russian artist Boris Lovet-Lorski taught A. L.'s daughter Marcella how to sculpt, in Paris in the 1920s, it was she who became responsible for orchestrating an exhibition of his works in the store's gallery in 1930. "Lorski used unusual media. That very fact made his contributions appropriate to the Gump's atmosphere. Like the cosmopolitan collections in the rest of the store, his marble had come from all over the world. There were only the finest Carrara from Italy, black marble from Belgium, and onyx from Mexico."

Lorski wrote to A. L. in 1933 asking if he could once again exhibit in the gallery. A. L. appreciated the sculptor's work and agreed, although he secretly harbored the fear that another exhibition of the highly priced works could be

risky. Advancing monies for the valuable artworks and arranging for an expensive hotel suite to entertain the artist paid off, however. His month-long show attracted over five thousand visitors. One of them, William Randolph Hearst, purchased a graceful silvery bronze statue seven and a half feet high for his San Simeon collection. A. L. was so pleased his instincts were right that he made arrangements for his grandchildren—still mere babes—to study with Lovet-Lorski as soon as they were old enough.

When Robert Gump's daughters were in grade school in the 1940s, A. L. thought that the educational system was not meeting the standards he had in mind for them. He wanted the children to study the classics and sent each child a carefully considered and specially tailored book list. Each granddaughter was not only expected to read the books but to write a book report on each and every title and send it to her grandfather. Although he was a very demanding patriarch, he could be kind and supportive. Marilyn wrote poetry as a teenager, and she sent a sample of it to her favorite grandfather. Without telling Marilyn, he sent it to Clare Booth Luce. A few days later, Luce sent her a telegram, congratulating her on her budding talents. Thus was the life of the mind in the circle of A. L.'s influence.

"MR. GUMP OF GUMP'S"

"Mr. A. L.," as he was called, or "Mr. Gump of Gump's," was always on hand during store hours, and he liked to be present whenever sales staff was waiting on customers—in every department. To that effect, he had a number of additional back stairways added to the interior of the Post Street building so he could appear just about anywhere posthaste. He was known for spending time explaining the history and symbolism of his wares.

Mr. Gump sold not only the objects themselves but the romance and mystique that went with them. He had a story to tell about every important item in the store. When a distinguished collector, such as Andrew Mellon or William Randolph Hearst, visited, he was a genial host. He asked questions in order to discover his guests' special interests and would entertain them with pertinent stories. Customers were flattered by this attention and told their friends not only to visit the store's beautiful rooms but to "be sure to see Mr. Gump."

S. & G. Gump's reputation for "high art" was not one A. L. took lightly. He continued to locate the very finest pieces, but some of them came to him in unprecedented ways. When still a young man apprenticed to his father he answered the request of an elderly French woman who wished to sell a work of art in order to return to France. As he climbed an old staircase in North Beach he had no idea the visit would end with him acquiring a masterpiece. "My dear sir, you are very young and this is a serious matter," the old woman greeted him with surprise. Ceremoniously removing a sheet that covered a grand canvas, she revealed a magnificent portrait of a reclining nude Empress Josephine of France by Baron Pascal de Girard. The painting, left to her by her father, a Parisian art dealer, had been saved when it and other such works were under order of destruction during the downfall of the Empire. He simply could not bring himself to ruin the painting, and keeping it for private enjoyment, reported it destroyed along with the others. A. L. realized this piece was definitely a prize, and he agreed to pay the woman the $700 she demanded. Collis Huntington later bought the picture for $7000, making the Gumps richer by 1000 per cent.

Generally speaking, A. L.'s reputation as a shrewd businessman was well deserved and unchallenged. But when he met the British actress Lily Langtry he was outdone. Langtry, whose eventual collection of crystal necklaces would come entirely from Gump's, had come to visit the jewelry department, and A. L. offered suitable attention. He handed her a magnificent jade necklace and, wanting to sell it to her, he uttered only seven words, which though they seemed innocuous would haunt him long afterwards. "Miss Lily, this necklace is for you." She replied, "Mr. Gump, this is the nicest gift anyone has ever given me," and seizing the moment and the necklace, put the jewels in her purse and walked out of the store.

THE JEWEL ROOM SAFE, C. 1930.

ROBERT GUMP

YOU ARE THE ROSE, YOU ARE THE ROCK

Who, then, can
hold this
world
as a rock, or
savor it
as a
rose?

Who can
bind the
rock or
bound the
rose?

Is
not a
prayer a
rock;
is
not an
ecstacy a
rose?

Robert Gump, who left the family business in the 1940s and spent many years in Mexico, was the author of *You are the Rose, You are the Rock: An Eastern Logic,* published in 1967. Long before Shirley MacLaine or other New Age seers and publishers had commercialized "channelling," Robert "translated" this poem from an unknown author who communicated it to him in 1954, when he was living on the edge of the Mojave Desert. The poem "intruded itself" into his mind during a Sunday afternoon picnic with twenty friends, and he wrote it down as it came to him. The power of the communication was so strong that the words "were flowing off the end of the pencil." After the spirit left he found the words obscure and unconnected, but several weeks later the first lines of the poem also "came" to him, and the opus continued to be communicated to him every morning after he had finished his coffee for the next nine months.

FROM THE LIBRARY
OF
ROBERT L. GUMP.

Transcribing the poem took such concentration that Gump often found himself in a fugue, or trancelike state. But by the time the work was complete it contained "esoteric thoughts, Hindu concepts, even Chinese word orders, which required him to research some of the Eastern terms and concepts. Fortunately for Robert, his travels in the Orient as a child and on behalf of the family store must have provided him with a background or at least familiarized him with certain Eastern precepts.

"Who and where is the communicator? I don't know. It is probable that he lives in that part of Asia where the frontiers of China, India and Tibet conjoin. . . . Some of that which it has been commanded to write is truly beyond my understanding. So I have no idea why this duty was required of me. But it has been enlightening to have carried out the task."

ROBERT AND SALLY

When Robert Gump married Sally Stanford, the infamous madam and later mayor of Sausalito, it created a tremendous uproar. The event warranted three pages in *Life* magazine at the same time General MacArthur was recalled by President Truman. Clearly, the Gump/Stanford marriage was newsworthy to *Life's* readers. When Robert's brother Richard heard about the marriage, he was in New York with his wife, Agnes. When he hung up the telephone, she asked him, "What's the matter? You look white as a sheet. You look like Robert had married Sally Stanford or something!"

To celebrate *Town and Country* magazine's publication of a feature article about Gump's based on its being named one of the world's three peerless luxury merchants, the management held a party at Trader Vic's. A cross section of San Francisco society was invited. An elderly Sally Stanford, whose name had been added to the guest list after some deliberation on the part of the store, got up from her hospital bed (she had recently suffered a heart attack) and appeared in a dramatic black gown and ropes of Gump's pearls, holding forth with a drink in one gnarled hand and a cigarette in the other. Some years later, when Sally died, a photograph of her appeared in a silver frame in the Gump's catalogue. There was no explanation, it was simply a sentimental good-bye. It generated hundreds of letters evenly divided between praise for the store and horror that she would have been so honored. But it was a typically San Francisco thing to do.

GUMP'S COMPANY PICNIC, C.1920.

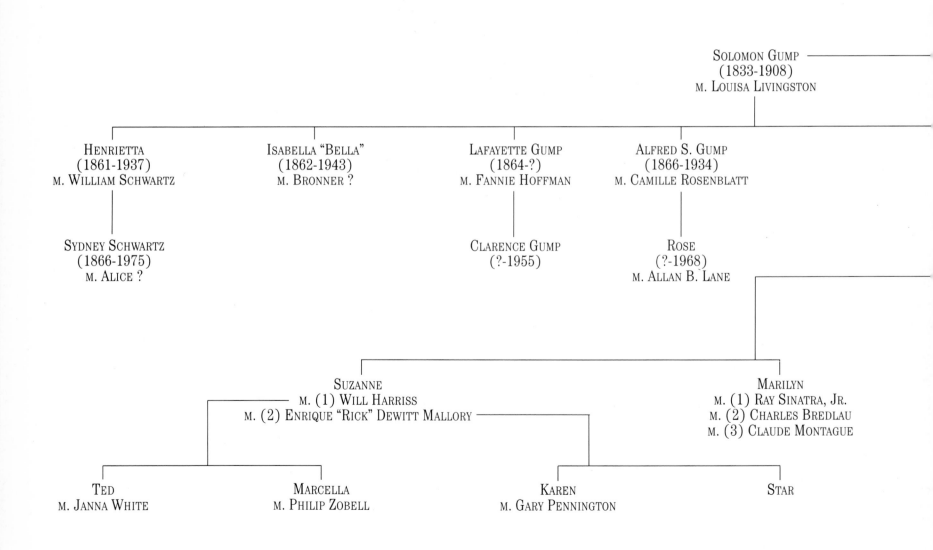

SOLOMON GUMP
(1833-1908)
M. LOUISA LIVINGSTON

HENRIETTA
(1861-1937)
M. WILLIAM SCHWARTZ

ISABELLA "BELLA"
(1862-1943)
M. BRONNER ?

LAFAYETTE GUMP
(1864-?)
M. FANNIE HOFFMAN

ALFRED S. GUMP
(1866-1934)
M. CAMILLE ROSENBLATT

SYDNEY SCHWARTZ
(1866-1975)
M. ALICE ?

CLARENCE GUMP
(?-1955)

ROSE
(?-1968)
M. ALLAN B. LANE

SUZANNE
M. (1) WILL HARRISS
M. (2) ENRIQUE "RICK" DEWITT MALLORY

MARILYN
M. (1) RAY SINATRA, JR.
M. (2) CHARLES BREDLAU
M. (3) CLAUDE MONTAGUE

TED
M. JANNA WHITE

MARCELLA
M. PHILIP ZOBELL

KAREN
M. GARY PENNINGTON

STAR

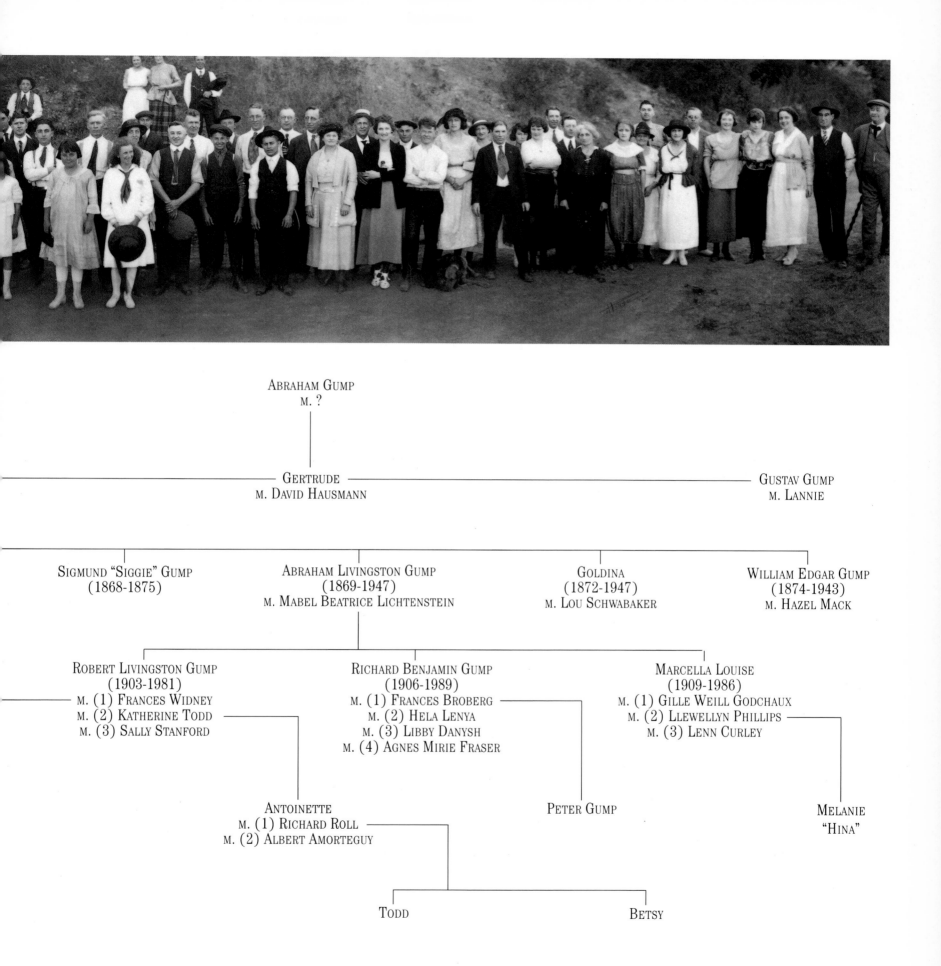

ABRAHAM GUMP
M. ?

GERTRUDE
M. DAVID HAUSMANN

GUSTAV GUMP
M. LANNIE

SIGMUND "SIGGIE" GUMP
(1868-1875)

ABRAHAM LIVINGSTON GUMP
(1869-1947)
M. MABEL BEATRICE LICHTENSTEIN

GOLDINA
(1872-1947)
M. LOU SCHWABAKER

WILLIAM EDGAR GUMP
(1874-1943)
M. HAZEL MACK

ROBERT LIVINGSTON GUMP
(1903-1981)
M. (1) FRANCES WIDNEY
M. (2) KATHERINE TODD
M. (3) SALLY STANFORD

RICHARD BENJAMIN GUMP
(1906-1989)
M. (1) FRANCES BROBERG
M. (2) HELA LENYA
M. (3) LIBBY DANYSH
M. (4) AGNES MIRIE FRASER

MARCELLA LOUISE
(1909-1986)
M. (1) GILLE WEILL GODCHAUX
M. (2) LLEWELLYN PHILLIPS
M. (3) LENN CURLEY

ANTOINETTE
M. (1) RICHARD ROLL
M. (2) ALBERT AMORTEGUY

PETER GUMP

MELANIE
"HINA"

TODD

BETSY

TESSIE WALL AND LADY LUCK

In the early 1900s, Tessie Wall, an entrepreneur in San Francisco's red light district, was a devotee of the Gump art collection and a frequent visitor to the store. She was mesmerized by a 17th Century painting depicting a salon where elegantly coiffed and gowned women reposed beneath a crystal chandelier. She just had to own it, but the $1000 price tag was not within her budget. Undaunted, and with a true San Francisco pioneer spirit, she told Willie Gump that she would go to the races and bet on a long shot. If she won, the painting would be hers. Lady Luck smiled on Tessie, and her horse won. When the young Gump arrived at her home to hang the painting, she paid him handsomely—in $20 gold pieces.

THE GALLERY

The Gump Gallery, opened by Solomon and Gustav, is the oldest art center in continuous operation in northern California. When the city of San Francisco settled down in the 1870s, its citizens began to think seriously about becoming educated in the ways of art and elegance. S. and G. had anticipated the trend toward fine art and were ready to meet their clients' demands for "high class" paintings to go into the frames they manufactured and sold. Solomon loved art and had already begun acquiring excellent contemporary pieces on his buying trips to Europe. Canvassing the Continent for great works, he returned laden with paintings, especially the pastorals and popular story paintings characteristic of the last half of the 19th Century. There was soon a constant flow of masterpieces into the Gallery, and they were quickly sold and proudly exhibited in the homes of the city's wealthy. The familiar names of Huntington, Coleman, and Spreckles appeared on S. & G. Gump Company invoices; huge canvases passed out of Gump's doors almost as fast as they came in.

With brilliant foresight, Gump's obtained the exclusive right to act as agent for Currier and Ives west of the Mississippi. (The prints were sold to customers for forty dollars each.) This was among the first steps toward a guaranteed successful artistic future for the young firm. Dealing in art proved to be so profitable that it necessitated a move to the more spacious quarters of the four-story Market Street building. Although the Gallery would be moved several more times, it found its permanent space on Post Street in 1909. As early as the late 1870s the Gallery featured works of representative American artists as well as famous continental masters.

The 1870s brought San Francisco the Palace, the Occidental, and other grand hotels whose interiors were finished and decorated with Gump's-commissioned mirrors, mouldings, and masterpieces. The vigorous bonanza on the Comstock led to the refurbishing of Virginia City by its renewed and new fortunes, with S. & G. Gump garnering bounteous commissions. During the same decade, William Marple, a local artist, entered into partnership with the Gumps, who in return for financial backing became the sole agent for his prize-winning and very-much-in-demand landscapes.

In the mid to late 1880s, when the Gallery was overstocked or when business lagged, Gump's held auctions, much to the delight of the gambling, fun-loving San Franciscans. Accompanying illustrated catalogues were written and printed with care. The auctions were integral to the Gallery's success in the early years because they allowed a large public forum to view and appreciate the variety and divergence of an attractive collection of art works. Prices ranged from $40 to $3000(today approximately $75 to $75,000), giving the public, well monied or not, the opportunity to own a piece of art.

As the artistic climate of San Francisco started to warm up, the daily papers covered the auctions at Gump's. "The auction sale of the Gump collection was, as a whole, rather more successful than had been expected, and will, it is hoped, induce the Messrs. Gump to continue the plan of importing first class European paintings to the city. The sale began on Wednesday evening and was continued thereafter afternoons and evenings through the week. The entire collection brought something more than $37,000, which is considered very fair." Indeed.

While the Gallery, throughout its history, brought Rembrandts, Renoirs, Matisses, and Corots to a tradition-bound San Francisco, the historically important function of the Gallery has been its role in supporting contemporary art. Among the artists it featured, when they were new and relatively unknown, were Albert Bierstadt, Thomas Hill, Maynard Dixon, Fletcher Benton, Nathan Oliveira, Wayne Thibaud, and Richard Diebenkorn. These and other artists subsequently became international names, but many others of talent and promise achieved lesser distinction. The Gallery always took risks, and ascribed to Gump's' overall charter to be an educational and uplifting experience as well as a retail establishment.

CHRIST IN GETHSEMANE

In 1887, John Zeile, a founding member of the San Francisco Art Association, bought the painting *Christ in Gethsemane* directly from its artist, Heinrich Hofmann, in his Dresden studio and brought it back to the West Coast. Fortunately, before the devastating fire after the 1906 earthquake, the painting was rescued. Just who, ly, was responsible for this heroic act is still a matter of controversy. Some accounts credit Zeile, "who ripped it from the frame and carried it to safety." But according to A. L. Gump, in an article written for *The Saturday Evening Post,* "…probably the most beautiful of all modern paintings of the Christ was rescued by William B. Faville, an architect, who had the good sense to cut the canvas from the frame, roll it up and take it across the Bay to Sausalito."

In 1930, Zeile offered the painting for public viewing in the store during Easter week. At the end of the week, he allowed Gump's to continue showing the portrait in the Art Gallery, thereby establishing "The Shrine" for many store patrons. Zeile sold the painting to Gump's and for five years it remained a significant draw. The companion pieces, *Christ and the Rich Young Ruler* and *The Image of Christ,* had previously found their home in Riverside Church in New York.

A special exhibit featuring the two paintings borrowed from the New York church, *Christ at Gethsemane*, and a fourth by Hofmann entitled *The Boy Christ* were exhibited in "The Shrine" for a number of weeks. A. L. was reluctant to sell *Christ in Gethsemane* until he was assured by philanthropist John D. Rockefeller (who had owned one of the triptych) that the painting would have an enormous audience in New York. He sold the painting to Rockefeller, who in turn donated it to Riverside Church, and the three Hofmann works were hung together.

ED NEWELL AND THE BIRTH OF THE JADE ROOM

Ed Newell was an acquaintance of Mabel and A. L.'s, who, as Shreve and Company's buyer for Oriental art and arti- facts, had travelled to Japan. He shared A. L.'s interest in and enthusiasm for beautiful things from Asia. When Shreve determined that the Oriental end of the art business was not where it intended to focus, Newell found himself jobless. A. L. took him on at Gump's to help get the store back to rights after the 1906 earthquake and help realize his vision of the future in Oriental trade. A third of the new store was made into an Oriental Room, where a few pieces were displayed on an altar Newell rescued from the ruins of a Buddhist temple in Chinatown. They also installed a Japanese Room on the second floor. Newell's experience in Japan had made him quite knowledgeable about the quality of Oriental goods, and he knew where to get his hands on some pieces from private collectors. Fur- thermore, his business activity in Japan had taught him to distinguish the shoddier goods made specifically for for- eign export from the real stuff.

Mabel and A. L. decided it was in the best interest of the store to send Newell to Japan once again. He renewed the contacts he had made on his first journey and went to remote villages, on long and arduous boat trips, and into the homes of the aristocracy to acquire merchandise to ship back to San Francisco. In some ways, this Gump-sponsored trip of Newell's was an experiment. He bought in odd quantities a number of unusual things—gold- en silk priest's robes, antique kimonos and obis from pawnshops and used clothing stores, and of course, the wood- block prints that were available in such abundance that the Japanese used them to wrap porcelain.

When he was ready to visit China in 1907, he had learned from his Japanese associates where to go and what to buy for how much and from whom. He went directly to the open port of Canton, where he stocked up on Chinese

THE JADE ROOM, c. 1908. DESIGNED BY
GUSTAVE LILJESTROM.

CARVED FROM A SINGLE PIECE OF
NEPHRITE, THIS CH'ING DYNASTY (1644-
1911) INCENSE BURNER WAS MADE TO
HONOR YU HUANG, THE JADE EMPEROR.
CHINESE FOLKLORE CHARACTERIZES YU
HUANG AS "THE GIVER OF LIFE, THE VITAL-
IZING POWER OF EARTH; JUDGE, FORGIVER
AND SAVIOUR OF MANKIND." THE PUNGENT
SMELL OF INCENSE WAS THOUGHT TO
PLEASE THE GODS AND DRIVE OFF EVIL
SPIRITS, WHILE THE SMOKE WAS BELIEVED
TO CARRY PRAYERS TO DIVINE EARS. ON
THE EIGHTH DAY OF THE FIRST MONTH,
PILGRIMS JOURNEYED TO THE TEMPLE OF
YU HUANG TO LIGHT CANDLES AND MAKE
OFFERINGS OF FRUIT AND INCENSE. THE
PRAYERS ACCOMPANYING THE SMOKE FROM
THIS MAGNIFICENT PIECE OF JADE WERE
CERTAINLY CONVEYED ALOFT.

furniture, embroidered linens, and "canton ware," porcelain manufactured in actuality closer to Shanghai but exported from Canton. In Shanghai he did not buy any jade, since America did not yet have an Eastern appreciation of the stone and the jewelry and carvings made from it. Instead he took richly colored bolts of silks and satins. Then he continued on to Peking.

Newell was one of the first (if not actually *the* first) of the buyers from the West Coast to enter the northern Chinese provinces. Until he arrived there he had no idea that Peking (Beijing) was the center of ancient Chinese culture. Previously, Newell had judged Chinese art only by what he had seen and bought in San Francisco, Canton, and Japan. He had never before encountered anything like the lacquered wood lamps, jade cups, or beautiful bronzes of Peking. Without experience at playing the Chinese business negotiation games, he was nearly at a loss. How would he ever purchase these amazing things from their owners and manufacturers? Fortunately, Newell's frank admiration of the works of art, his obvious ingenuousness and his willingness to play straight, no tricks, led the Chinese merchants to deal fairly with him for the most part. But because he was reluctant to sink any of A. L.'s money into a shipment of goods about which he knew little and for which he was uncertain a market existed at home, Newell did not show a readiness to spend and was not always shown top merchandise. He bought what the Peking underground called "mixed cargo," an assortment of brasses, Mandarin robes, and a small selection of old porcelain—no one item over $100—and returned to California.

The day that the shipment arrived from China, Ed and A. L. hastened down to the storeroom and excitedly raised the lid on the first crate. What they found was a jumbled mess of broken porcelain. Although Newell had hired professional packers, he had overlooked the matter of customs inspection and tax. He did not arrange for personal supervision of the shipment at the port of Tientsin, and the customs officials cared little for the fragility of the cargo. But Lady Luck paid a visit to Gump's in the personage of Mrs. Francis Carolan (whose fortune came from the Pullman railroad car company) while Ed and A. L. dejectedly picked their way through the shards. Mrs. Carolan had

developed an interest in Chinese art in Paris, and on hearing that there was a new shipment of pieces from the northern provinces, she took all the unbroken ones!

When Ed Newell visited Canton he went to Jade Street, the center of the jade trade in China, but he didn't buy a single piece, under the impression that "there wouldn't be any interest in jade at home." When he returned to Japan, however, he fell captive to the lure of the mysterious stone. He found himself in a small shop where the proprietor, an elderly gentleman, showed him a pair of magnificent white jade vases carved in the design of old bronzes of the pre-Christian era. "The carving was superb and I hadn't known that such pieces existed. Never had I seen anything like this in China." When he asked the price he was completely unprepared for the answer—each vase cost several thousand dollars. The equivalent sum today would be close to a quarter million dollars.

Unsure that Gump's could sell the vases, he was somewhat averse to purchasing them. The price was also of significant consideration. But he weakened and fell victim to "jade madness," acquiring the vases that had been a gift to the shogun of Japan from the emperor in the 18th Century. When A. L. saw the vases in San Francisco, Newell was confident he had made the proper decision in buying them. "I think that single purchase gave us both an insight into what the future might hold for fine jade." It also provided inspiration for Gump's famed Jade Room.

Gustave Liljestrom, a former teacher at the Art Institute of Chicago and resident designer of Oriental interiors for the store and its patrons, drew up the plans for the Jade Room. It had high ceilings and floor space for a single table and four chairs. Along three walls, deep recessed showcases held the precious jades behind walnut doors carved with Chinese symbols. Through this room would pass thousands of visitors, including many of the world's most notable jade collectors. On display was an ever-changing assembly of the finest examples of the jade carver's art, at times exceeding a million dollars in value, by 1908 standards. Since its appearance, the Jade Room has provided an opportunity for millions of people, some of them for the first time, to see jade and vow to possess some day "a piece of Heaven."

PIECES OF THE PAST

THE LOGO

In 1866, the company was known as S. & G. Gump Company, Fine Arts, named after its founders, Solomon and Gustav Gump. Their letterhead logo depicted a muse with a painter's palette seated on a pediment decorated with crests and swags beneath an arch of Greek key devices.

In 1932, Richard Gump, a noted designer and painter in his own right, created a new logo for the store, employing a streamlined modern typeface. He had the logo reproduced in chrome letters affixed to the store's delivery trucks. This signature was so simple, attractive, and evocative that it remains virtually unchanged today, some sixty years later.

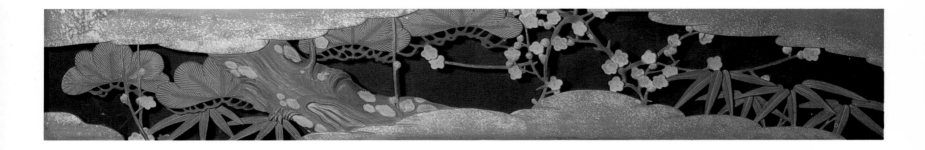

THE FOUR VASES

Schuyler Parsons was one of the foremost art dealers of the 1920s. Always on the lookout for one-of-a-kind pieces for his clients, when one of his wealthy customers asked him to go to San Francisco to "that great art store," Gump's, he agreed. The client wanted him to look at four Chinese vases, and told him if he liked their color to telephone for immediate authorization of the sale.

In San Francisco, Parsons met with A. L. Gump and was shown the four exquisite vases. "I never saw anything finer in form, color or contour," Parsons later noted, and he made the telephone call. What he didn't realize was that A. L. had already put the vases "on hold" for his own privileged client, Colonel Jackling, the founder of the Utah Copper Company and one of the "truly towering magnificoes of the 20th Century." Jackling wanted the vases for his palatial estate in Hillsborough, California. A. L. knew he had a sale, but to which customer?

Parsons and Jackling bid fast and furiously for four days and the telephone wires sizzled with the negotiations. At the end of day four Parsons was authorized to bid $105,000 for his client, but the colonel offered $110,000—more than one million dollars by today's standards—and the vases were his.

GUMP'S FIRST FLOOR, C.1925.

TEXTURE

❖ The shimmer of a perfect pearl ❖
❖ the gleam of molten gold ❖
❖ the cool of water jade ❖
❖ the warmth of an old Tabriz ❖
❖ the fragrance of fresh-cut lilacs ❖
❖ the drama of cast bronze ❖
❖ the clarity of a rare emerald ❖
❖ the satin smoothness of old mahogany ❖
❖ the melody of a trickling fountain ❖
❖ the translucence of fine porcelain ❖
❖ the bell-like ring of lead crystal ❖
❖ the scent of potpourri ❖
❖ the resonance of a bronze temple bell ❖

"ALL THESE WORDS MEET VIOLENTLY TO FORM A texture both impressive and exciting," wrote Poet Laureate John Berryman to describe the identifying quality of poetry. The identifying quality of Gump's lies also in its richly endowed texture. Its very essence is in the sight, sound, touch, and smell of all its inviting objects. To enter is to partake of a feast for the senses.

GOLD AND PEARLS: RANSOMS FIT FOR KINGS AND QUEENS

Gold and pearls—symbols of the sun and the moon—are the stars of Gump's Jewel Room. It's fitting that a store that's grown up in San Francisco over the past 130-plus years should feature fine gold jewelry and superb pearls. Gold was at the base of San Francisco's foundation. Pearls reflect Gump's long and close association with Oriental culture, art, and beauty.

Gold brought thousands of adventurers from around the world to the California port in the Gold Rush of 1849, to pursue their dreams in the Sierras. Some struck it rich and returned to the city by the Bay with a gold craze still in their hearts. The kings of California's Mother Lode in 1849 and Nevada's Comstock Lode ten years later built Victorian palaces adorned with gilt and gold leaf. And all that glittered was supplied by Gump's.

Today, Gump's gold is less ostentatious. Tasteful, top-quality gold jewelry is featured in Gump's collection of exquisite fourteen- and eighteen-carat gold; necklaces, bracelets, brooches, rings, and earrings, including pieces set with diamonds and other precious stones. There are gold cuff links, tie and money clips, gold ball point pens. All that glitters at Gump's is fit for a modern king or queen.

Gold has been associated with royalty for millenia. Gold in ancient Egypt was the property of the pharaohs, who linked gold to Ra, God of the Golden Sun, the giver of life. Goldsmiths created golden objects to meet the needs of the boy king Tutankhamen who died in 1350 B.C. He was entombed with gold crowns, bracelets, amulets, chariots, and a throne.

Sixteenth Century Spanish conquistadors acting on King Ferdinand's orders to "Forget spices—get gold!" plundered the New World to fill Spain's coffers. In South America, El Dorado, "the gilded man," was worshipped by the Chibeha Indians as their Sun God in an extravagant rite that took place every year. As the sun rose above the Andes the king-priest plastered with gold dust was floated on a barge to the center of Lake Guatavita, where he plunged into the sacred water. Natives tossed gold images, beads, and nuggets around him. El Dorado!

In their search for El Dorado, Spaniards captured Atibaliba, the Inca chief, and Montezuma, the Aztec king. In their search for El Dorado, the place of gold, they looted an estimated thirteen tons of golden artifacts. The treasures were melted into ingots to simplify transporting the booty back to Spain. El Dorado!

Gump's Jewel Room—a modern El Dorado—contains gold jewelry that's as bold and exciting as a thunderbolt, as dainty and strong as a cobweb in the morning sun. Gold is a metal for all seasons. The golden rule of fashion is that there are no rules for gold. Gold goes anywhere: to the office, to the opera, to sporting events, to the beach.

Gump's treasure contains finely crafted fourteen-carat link and braided gold necklaces. Dangling pendants and lockets of gold adorned with enamel and jewels are as gay as Christmas ornaments, luxurious German-crafted baubles inspired by 19th Century designs. There are smooth gold and twisted gold bangle bracelets, and myriad knot and hoop earrings in traditional and modern designs. Gump's special collection of eighteen-carat polished or brushed gold brooches is a menagerie of golden tigers, giraffes, and elephants to brighten lapels. A racing roadrunner with an emerald eye is a favorite. There are frogs, bees, and a gold and green enamel cricket. For lovers of the sea there are otters and dolphins, a crab with a diamond in its pincers, a ruby-eyed octopus. There's something for every taste in Gump's special cache of gold.

Outside San Francisco's Golden Gate another treasure lay in the waters of the Pacific that stretch to Asia and the South Seas. After the 1906 earthquake Gump's looked to the Orient for new and exciting goods. It found exotic art, delicate porcelains, bronzes, jades, and lucious pearls.

The pearl was known in Sanskrit as *sasi-rana,* or gem of the moon. The lustrous white spheres, as mysterious as the celestial bodies they resemble, are as irresistible to us today as they were to monarchs in days gone by.

It's suspected that Julius Caesar, who was particularly fond of pearls, invaded Britain with the hope of finding freshwater pearls, which had come from the rivers in the British Isles for two thousand years. Meanwhile Mark

PREVIOUS SPREAD: THE UNUSUAL SHAPES OF FRESHWATER PEARLS LEND THEMSELVES TO DELIGHTFULLY IMAGINATIVE DESIGNS. THE BEAUTY OF THE FRESHWATER PEARL HAS STIMULATED THE DEVELOPMENT OF FARMS IN JAPAN, NOTABLY AROUND LAKE BIWA, THE SOURCE OF THE LARGE MUSSELS WHOSE INTERIORS REVEALED THE BRONZE-COLORED PEARLS IN THIS STRAND. THEIR UNIQUE BEAUTY MAKES THEM A SOUGHT-AFTER PRIZE ALL OVER THE WORLD.

RIGHT: THE VALUE OF SEMIPRECIOUS STONES HAS VARIED OVER THE YEARS, FROM TIME TO TIME AND PLACE TO PLACE. THESE SEMIPRECIOUS STONES ARE DISPLAYED TO GREATEST ADVANTAGE IN GOLD AND DIAMOND SETTINGS CREATED EXCLUSIVELY FOR GUMP'S BY THE STORE'S JEWELRY DEPARTMENT DESIGNERS.

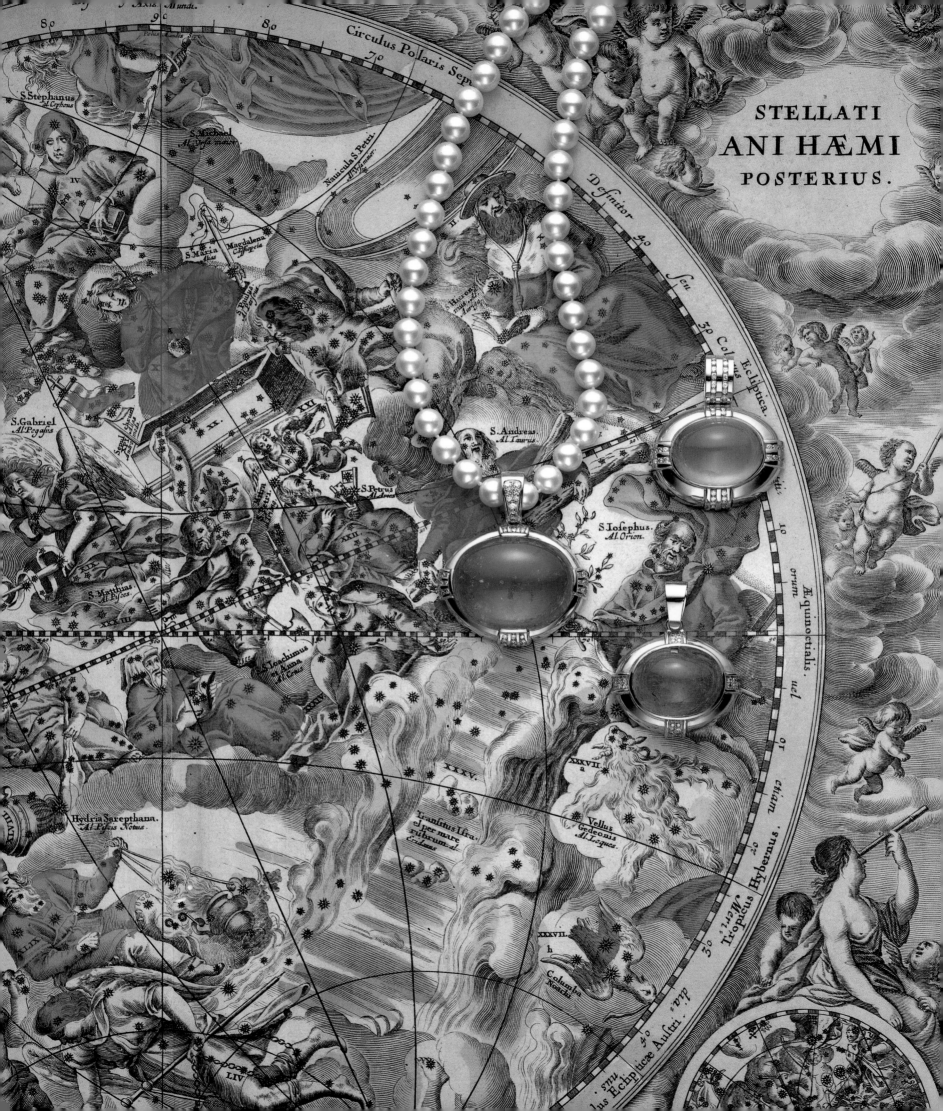

Anthony, legend has it, was quaffing wine laced with crushed pearl. Cleopatra's cocktail was reputed to be an aphrodisiac that would inspire eternal love.

Centuries later pearls symbolized power and far-flung empire. Henry VIII of England and Francis I of France were sartorial as well as political rivals. Each tried to outdo the other with extravagant pearl jewelry and pearl-encrusted costumes.

Elizabeth I shared her father's penchant for pearls. Mary, Queen of Scots, erred when she offered Elizabeth pearls that had belonged to her mother, Catherine de Medici, in exchange for keeping her head. Mary lost both.

In the East, sultans and maharajas entwined themselves with pearls retrieved from the Persian Gulf and the Red Sea by enslaved divers.

In 1893 an event occurred in the coastal town of Toba, Japan, that would eventually mean that virtually anyone, not only the rich and the royal, could wear pearls.

After years of struggle Kokichi Mikimoto, a Japanese noodle maker who had seeded thousands of oysters with dreams of creating a pearl, finally succeeded. A new phenomenon, the cultivated pearl, was born. By the 1920s cultured pearls were on the market, pearl farming was a new industry in Japan, and Mikimoto, a national hero, was crowned "the Pearl King."

Gump's pearls are among the finest to be found anywhere. There are ropes of round Japanese pearls and multi-strand chokers made with freshwater pearls from Lake Biwa and rivers in the Orient. There's jewelry made with large pearls called South Seas that are grown in Australia and black pearls from the South Pacific. There are baroque pearls, flat one-sided gems.

Gump's has a unique selection of clasps: tourmaline, antique carved jade, amethyst, and aquamarine, carved into melon, seashell, and other exotic shapes, or buff cut—cabochon on top, facets below—to show the color.

Myth and history, fantasy and romance surround Gump's gold and pearls. There's magic in Gump's Jewel Room and excitement in the air where the display cases glow with shining pieces of the golden sun and pearl drops from the moon.

NAN BIRMINGHAM

The jewelry department once had a perfect single, irridescent South Sea pearl that measured eighteen to twenty millimeters in size and was priced at a staggering $20,000. When it was put on sale it found a home within one week. A new South Sea pearl of similar description has been placed on sale in Gump's Jewel Room, priced at $75,000.

"Oh, you know, when it comes to pearls, it is very seldom that there isn't some shady story behind them."

OPPOSITE PAGE: JADE AND PEARLS—A DIVINE MARRIAGE OF ELEGANCE AND TASTE. PEARLS, LIKE JADE, HAVE ENJOYED AN ELUSIVE YET ROMANTIC ASSOCIATION AND HAVE BEEN COVETED BY ROYALTY BECAUSE OF THEIR PROTECTIVE CHARMS. THE HINDUS BELIEVED THAT THE GOD KRISHNA DISCOVERED THE PEARL WHEN HE PLUCKED IT FROM THE OCEAN AS AN ADORNMENT FOR HIS DAUGHTER ON HER WEDDING DAY. RED-HAIRED ELIZABETH I OF ENGLAND, HENRY VIII'S DAUGHTER, WAS THE FIRST TO WEAR A STRING OF PEARLS.

LEFT: GUMP'S' REPUTATION FOR PEERLESS PEARLS IS OWED IN PART TO THE EFFORTS OF ADA AMOROSA, PICTURED AT WORK. MRS. AMOROSA, GUMP'S' PEARL STRINGER, HAS BEEN AT THE STORE FOR OVER TWENTY-FIVE YEARS. WHEN DESIGNER AND GEM BUYER MARILU KLAR RETURNS FROM JAPAN WITH HER SELECTION OF PRIZED PEARLS, THEY ARE STRUNG AND KNOTTED ON SILK THREAD. COCO CHANEL, THE HIGH PRIESTESS OF CHIC, RECOGNIZED EARLY ON THAT WEARING PEARLS WAS NOT JUST STYLISH, IT WAS THE EPITOME OF STYLE.

JADE

Jade is a possession to be cherished by anyone who can find it or buy it or steal it. Chinese women ask for jade ornaments for their hair and old men keep in their closed palms a piece of cool jade, so smooth that it seems soft to the touch. Rich men buy jades instead of putting their money in banks, for jade grows more beautiful with age. When men die, their families put jade in the tombs with them to keep them from decay. The poorest courtesan had her bit of jade —to hang in her ears or to use in a hairpin, and the most successful and popular actresses wear jade instead of diamonds, because jade is the most sumptuous jewel against a woman's flesh.

PEARL S. BUCK

WITH A LOOK AS SOFT AS MOULDED CLOUDS, THESE JADE NECKLACES MAKE A SUMPTUOUS DISPLAY. PERHAPS THE MOST FAMOUS "QUEEN OF JADE" WAS YANG KUEIFEI, MISTRESS OF THE CHINESE EMPEROR MING HUANG. HER SKIN WAS AS WHITE AND SMOOTH AS JADE AND HER FEATURES WERE AS FINELY CARVED AS JADE. SHE BECAME KNOWN AS THE JADE BEAUTY, AND LEGEND HAS IT THAT SHE SLEPT ON A JADE BED, WORE ONLY JADE ORNAMENTS AND SURROUNDED HERSELF WITH ONLY JADE OBJECTS. FROM HER ROBES HUNG A LARGE VARIETY OF TASSELLED JADES; FROM HER WAIST HUNG A SMALL JADE CYLINDER THAT CONTAINED THE FRAGRANCE OF BLOSSOMS. IN HER LONG BLACK HAIR SHE WORE TWO JADE HAIRPINS. FAVORING SMALL PENDANTS IN MYRIAD COLORS, ELABORATE EARRINGS, BRACELETS, AND BROOCHES (ALL OF JADE), THE QUEEN OF JADE WAS AN EXQUISITE MODEL FOR SUCH A PRECIOUS STONE.

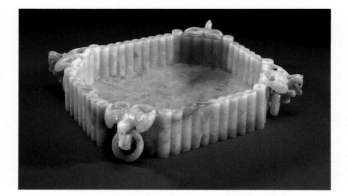

JADE, STONE OF HEAVEN

If a stone could speak, what a story jade would tell! It might speak of the primitive, perhaps even savage man who first discovered and used jade, and of how he set a pattern that all men would follow of seeing in the stone that which he most needed and desired. For him it was toughness and strength. For others, it would be beauty, noble thought, usefulness, decoration, a path to the Divine.

Jade held a special place in Chinese religion, a place accorded no other substance. It was the link between earth and heaven, the bridge from life to immortality. It was a conduit, a conductor, the embodiment of man's highest thought, just touching upon the Divine. In religious ceremonies, the emperor often used jade as we might a telephone, except that he held up the jade form and spoke through it, to heaven. And through jade, heaven was said to send its blessings in return.

Confucians carried jade to purify the mind, to awaken inspiration. Taoists called it yang, the male creative principle, since in its purest form it resembled the seed of man and was said to contain the potentialities of all life, both human and Divine.

The hues of jade were more than colors to the ancient Chinese. Five, in their purity, represented nature's basic elements. Yellow = earth. Black = water. White = air or metal. Red = fire. Green = wood. Its color represents loyalty; its interior flaws, always showing themselves through the transparency, call to mind sincerity; its iridescent brightness represents the heavens; its admirable substance, born of mountain and water, represents the earth. Used alone or without ornamentation it represents chastity. The price which all the world attaches to it represents truth. The Chinese consider it their most sacred gift, believing that in giving jade, they are giving a part of themselves.

Jade carving differs from other arts, just as jade differs from other stones. Jade was believed to be the essence of creation; all that existed was believed to be latent, embodied in the stone itself. The craftsman in bronze, the landscape painter, the ceramic potter used their arts to portray life as they saw it within traditional forms. But the attitude of the jade carver was different. He did not seek to convey a philosophy, but to reveal it. He carved to bring out the symbols of nature, the patterns of the universe that were inherent in jade.

If jade is highly valued it is because, since ancient times, the wise have likened it to virtue. For them, its polish and brilliancy represent the whole of purity, its perfect compactness and extreme hardness represent the sureness of intelligence; its angles, which do not cut, although they seem sharp, represent justice; the pure and the prolonged sound which it gives forth when one strikes it represents music.

There is a magic about jade that seems to elude man's definition, that sets it apart from all other stones. A mystery that lies beyond man's appreciation of its rarity or the skillful carving of its surface; that entices and comes closest to revealing itself when man handles "the stone of heaven." A special, hidden beauty that causes men, when they speak of jade, to speak in the language of myth and legend. Ordinary words are limited; the special quality within in the jade stone is not.

RICHARD GUMP

MARILU KLAR, CURATOR OF GEMS

As curator of the prestigious jewelry department, Marilu Klar has scoured the world for over two decades in search of perfect gemstones. Hired by store president Richard Gump in the early 1960s, Klar was told that she, like all other potential employees, had to pass the "good taste test," a rigid requirement. But Klar, a woman of exceptional taste—and tasteful exception—told Gump directly, "I don't need taste, Mr. Gump, I already have it." She certainly did.

Logging a formidable number of miles across the globe, Klar has been instrumental in helping create and uphold the Jewelry Department's impeccable reputation. Securing and maintaining relationships with gem sellers the world over, Klar's business acumen is most discerning. She is scrupulous in her purchase of pearls, jades, corals, or colored stones, and has been known to sit for hours sorting stones, looking for "just the right light."

Her resolve not only to design the best but to purchase the best has placed her in some unusual circumstances. She has trekked through the snows of Moscow and weathered the intense heat of the Far East. One of the first women to conduct business in male-dominated Asian countries, Klar is a redoubtable trader. She prides herself

THE TRUE PURPOSE OF LUXURY CANNOT BE ANY
OTHER THAN TO MAKE SIMPLICITY APPEAR
REMARKABLE. THESE SEMIPRECIOUS GEMSTONE
PENDANTS SET IN GOLD AND DIAMONDS POSSESS
A CERTAIN TIMELESS DESIGN THAT IS MOST
APPEALING. IN THE 1900s, AT THE BEGINNING
OF THE BELLE EPOCH, SEMIPRECIOUS STONES
WERE USED IN JEWELRY DESIGN AND THE POPU-
LARITY OF DIAMONDS WANED. ECONOMY OF
DESIGN HAS ALWAYS BEEN THE APPROACH OF
JEWELRY DESIGNERS JOHN HORNUNG AND
MARILU KLAR. WHEN THE GEMSTONES ARE AS
SPECIAL AS THESE PICTURED, THE INHERENT
BEAUTY OF THE STONES SPEAKS FOR ITSELF.
ELEGANCE IS ALWAYS IN FASHION.

on her "only the best" philosophy, subscribing to A. L. Gump's own credo. In fact, many of the dealers she conducts business with have been selling to Gump's since A. L.'s days.

If Klar's well-trained eye is a sophisticated one, and surely it is, this may well be due to her artistic background. She studied art history at the University of California at Berkeley and was trained as a colorist at the Rudolph Schaeffer School of Design in San Francisco.

Jewelry customers usually return to Gump's year after year, purchasing new treasures and passing down their pieces from mother to daughter to granddaughter. Sometimes they select new pieces and other times they seek to update a look from the past. "Most of our customers are loyal. We don't have many customers who never return. We are always prepared to work with them and we like to think that we have collectors rather than just customers. With each generation, taste changes a little, but not really that radically. The granddaughter can still wear something made for her grandmother."

One of Ms. Klar's creative opportunities presented itself when a loyal customer brought in a large number of pieces she never wore. Her husband had bought them for her over the years, but she thought they weren't contemporary enough. Klar explained, "We took all of the old opals out of a pair of earrings and we took some jade out of a bracelet and selected a beautiful eighteen-carat cuff to create a magnificent bracelet. It was very exciting and makes the jewelry much more meaningful."

Klar has an admirable working relationship with designer John Hornung, who has also been affiliated with the Jewelry Department for many years. As they have worked together over time, they have become aware of each other's taste and Klar has been afforded the confidence of knowing inherently what type of jewelry Hornung will design for the stones she has purchased. It's almost as if Marilu is the left hand and John is the right hand, working in tandem. "He is really wonderful; we work together so well that we hardly have to say anything. I will buy something and I just know what he will do."

Klar's metier has brought her challenges and a great deal of enjoyment and satisfaction. She looks forward to many more years with the store. After all, travelling all over the world in quest of its most beautiful gems is hardly a vocation one tires of easily.

JANET LYNN ROSEMAN

THE ADVENTURES OF MARILU KLAR

Travelling throughout the world to choose wonderful things has been an extraordinary life's work. In this role, Marilu has had to be both the gracious guest and the knowledgeable buyer. Once, looking for pearls, she was shown to a table in a dimly lit room. "Trays of pearls were served to me as though they were something delicious to eat. I might have been able to eat in that setting but it was far too dark to judge the pearls. I wound up on my knees in front of the window with the trays of pearls spread out before me, sorting them. Politely, of course."

Her memories of back alleys in Hong Kong include long climbs up the narrow staircases of disreputable-looking buildings in dangerous neighborhoods to find some perfect jades. She went places no Westerner and certainly no woman was expected to go. And what she found was inevitably worth the uncertainty.

In different countries around the world Ms. Klar experienced a diverse range of receptions. "Sometimes I was treated like visiting royalty and other times I was simply ignored. I loved the stories that accompanied the antique jewels and precious stones I was shown. And there were always surprises. I was often surprised by extensive ceremony involved in the displaying and praising of the jewel broker's wares. Sometimes the surprise was on the seller's face when he realized that the Gump's buyer was me. All five feet and 100 pounds of me!"

After many years of working with the Japanese pearl sellers, Marilu was invited to attend an important annual August festival. A complete traditional Japanese costume—under kimono, outer kimono, haori, socks, obi, high platform geta, and all the other pieces of the getup—was delivered to her hotel. While her hosts expected her to wear this outfit, she had no idea how to put it on. "The chambermaids and hotel secretaries had a wonderful time dressing me up properly. Eventually, when I was escorted into the street in the blinding summer sun, I put on my sunglasses. I apparently looked so authentic that tourists descended upon me with requests to take my picture—until I took my glasses off. "

"One must live with a piece of jade to fully appreciate its majesty. The stone promises to slowly reveal its secret to its appointed owner" (Jade: Stone of Heaven). The Chinese believed that "feeling jade" enables its owner to truly know it. Jade served as a powerful bridge between this world and the next.

SHOPPING IN THE ORIENT

Ed Newell, in his capacity as chief buyer for Oriental goods, made many trips to Japan during his long career at the store. His uncanny business sense brought the riches of Nippon to Gump's for years. During one buying trip in Kyoto, the country's center of art and culture, Newell admired a small bronze statue. When he inquired about the price, he was told it was a modest 10 yen. He agreed to purchase the statue and asked the price for replicating it by the dozen. The craftsman told him it would be 150 yen per dozen. Newell protested; according to his calculations, 12 times 10 is only 120 yen. The artist replied, "Yes, I know. But if I make one, that is a pleasure. If twelve, I get tired and lose interest. Anyway, if you want them that badly you should be willing to pay more for them." Newell did.

FOLLOWING IN ED NEWELL'S FOOTSTEPS, GUMP'S VICE PRESIDENT MARTIN ROSENBLATT TRAVELLED TO CHINA AND JAPAN TO FIND UNIQUE MERCHANDISE FOR THE STORE.

SHOPPING AT GUMP'S

She's a world class shopper. You know the kind. Ten minutes in town and she knows exactly where to go for everything special and just when to go there. When she arrives in a new city, she's bound to find something special. With stately focus, gleeful anticipation, and matchless enthusiasm, she heads out of her hotel room knowing the pleasure of the chase will end well. In San Francisco she found Gump's and learned what generations of San Franciscans have always known. Gump's is it, the perfect store. No surprise to hear it's now her favorite store.

Her collection of Gumpiana has grown over the years. There's the Imari ashtray she got for her husband's office. Two Mary Tifit prints hang in the second bedroom in the country house. A family of bronze cranes nest in the backyard shrubbery. Family milestones have been marked with Gump's gifts: the cufflinks for her elder son's thirtieth birthday; her younger son's leather card case upon graduation from business school; a silver rattle on the arrival of grandbaby Alixandra; and a water jade ring for her mother. A growing collection of Herend fills a faux bamboo étagere and a select number of ceramic novelty vases hold her garden's seasonal offerings. Invitations to weddings and baby showers send her to the phone to place orders for Baccarat decanters and baby-sized china decorated with Babar the Elephant. She is surrounded at home with reminders of Gump's, from the Chinese roof tile sculpture on the coffee table to the tiny bronze rabbit box with a stomach full of stamps on her desk.

In the store there are a few items she only visits, like the platinum freshwater pearls from Lake Biwa in the Jewelry Department and the antique silver collection on the second floor, but that's all the more reason for her to go to Gump's. She'd really love to have the Buddha but it's too big to take home and it is *not* for sale ... not today, anyway, she says.

SUSAN KOHL

THIS EXCLUSIVE ORNAMENTAL ROOF TILE IS A REPRODUCTION OF THE ONES THAT ONCE GRACED THE ROOFTOPS OF CHINA'S OLDEST TEMPLES AND PALACES. CRAFTSMAN K. Y. LIN HAS SPENT A LIFETIME STUDYING THE LOST TEMPLE ART OF YEH WANG. THE MYSTERY OF ROOF TILE DESIGN HAS BEEN PASSED DOWN FROM ONE GENERATION TO ANOTHER SINCE THE MING DYNASTY (1368-1644). MR. LIN HAS PRESERVED THIS CHINESE FOLK ART, INTEGRATING THE TRADITIONAL STYLES OF THE PAST WITH HIS OWN CONTEMPORARY INNOVATIONS. HIS KNOWLEDGE AND EXPERIENCE SPAN MORE THAN THIRTY YEARS, AND HE HAS PERFECTED HIS OWN SECRET GLAZING METHOD FOR THESE CHINESE ANTEFIXES.

PREVIOUS SPREAD: THESE ONE-OF-A-KIND PERFUME BOTTLES ARE CARVED FROM NATURAL CRYSTAL. CAPPED WITH EIGHTEEN-CARAT GOLD, A ROW OF SAPPHIRES, AND CABOCHON EMERALDS, THEY ARE A SPLENDID EXAMPLE OF THE ARTISTRY BEFITTING THE MAGIC AND MYSTIQUE OF PERFUME.

RIGHT: LITHOGRAPH "MAN" BY NATHAN OLIVEIRA, 1989.

RECOLLECTIONS: 125 YEARS OF CALIFORNIA ARTISTS AT GUMP'S

The Art Gallery has presented the works of contemporary California artists since its opening. At the 1986 retrospective Recollections, the store offered public viewing of seventy-five paintings, watercolors, and graphic works by the artists who had exhibited at Gump's.

Art work in this special exhibition provided a rich survey of the development of art in California, spanning many different movements and styles. The earliest years were represented by William Keith and Thomas Hill, whose landscapes are classical yet romantic records of the West. This traditional viewpoint was continued by Percy Gray's local northern California landscapes and Charles Dorman Robinson's paintings of Mount Tamalpais and its views. Shortly after the turn of the century the influence of the Impressionists was apparent. European-trained Armin Hansen was among the first to capture everyday life, especially that of the waterfront, with a new palette. Post-Impressionists and Realists painted simultaneously, experimenting with subject matter and fresh colors. These were the years of Maynard Dixon's portraits, Arthur Matthews' *Carmel Valley*, the work of Helen Bruton, Frank Van Slous, and Lillie Mae Nicholson. The 1920s saw the advent of the "Society of Six," represented by East Bay artist Selden Connor Gile and his Marin County still lifes. Works by his colleagues Maurice Logan and Louis Siegrist, who were among the "plein-air" artists of the period, were also exhibited. Postwar years brought dramatic changes and innovations, seen in the art of today's gifted painters Morris Graves, Bryan Wilson, Robert Motherwell, Nathan Oliveira, Wayne Thiebaud, and Richard Diebenkorn, all of whom have been represented at Gump's.

A. L. and his son Richard developed a particular philosophy regarding art and taste that guided their acquisition of art works for sale in the Gallery and throughout the store. These insightful "Gumpisms" are still pertinent.

"A connoisseur will look for a good painting first and consider the artist's name second."

"Most artists have their inspired moments and their bad days. Any picture dealer or alert gallery-goer knows that the work of nearly every well-known artist is not uniform. And though the name is A-1, the painting may be 4-F."

"It is not the medium that makes a worthwhile picture. Because of the materials and techniques involved, it takes a longer time to produce an oil painting than a watercolor or drawing. But the artist working in oils can make mistakes and alterations that would ruin a watercolor. It is a foolish pretense to think that an oil painting is better, assuming both are of the same caliber."

"A true artist does not belabor his public with the painstaking effort and study necessary to produce his work. We know that Rembrandt was a great technician and a tormented man, but when we see one of his best canvasses, we feel power and inspiration, not weeks of hard, sad labor."

"Fondness for the erstwhile possessions of someone else may be born of a documentary fascination and make no sense for beauty's sake....Except for jewels and ornaments of definite worth, it is a waste of time and money to buy anything simply because its former owner was a famous figure."

RIGHT: THE DAVID HOCKNEY SHOW PROVIDED A CONTEMPORARY COUNTERPOINT TO THE EXHIBIT OF WINSTON CHURCHILL'S PAINTINGS DURING THE "BRITISH STYLE" SHOW OF 1985.

OPPOSITE PAGE: DANTE MARIONI'S HAND-BLOWN GLASS VASES ARE DISTINCTIVE AND WHIMSICAL. HE CALLS THE LARGER PIECES "WHOPPERS" AND THE SMALLER ONES "NOT-SO-WHOPPERS." HIS CAREFULLY CRAFTED GLASS-WARE IS REMINISCENT OF CLASSICAL FORMS IN PRAISE OF THE GODS. MARIONI HAS RECEIVED A NUMBER OF HONORS, INCLUDING THE PRESTI-GIOUS LOUIS COMFORT TIFFANY AWARD AND AWARDS FROM THE AMERICAN CRAFT MUSEUM AND THE NEW YORK EXPERIMENTAL GLASS WORKSHOP. THE COLLECTIONS OF THE CORNING MUSEUM OF GLASS, THE NATIONAL GALLERY OF VICTORIA IN AUSTRALIA, AND THE PRESCOTT COLLECTION IN SEATTLE ALL BOAST SAMPLES OF HIS ART, AS DOES GUMP'S GALLERY, VOLUME II.

THE PERFECT EYE

In a tumultuous world of grand egos, fervent competition, and artistic frenzy sits Helen Heninger, calm and composed. When her reign as director of Gump's Gallery came to an end in 1990, she merely exchanged one dream job for another. Now she oversees the Gump's Gallery, Volume II, canvassing the United States for new pieces of American craft art. For over three decades, this California native has been responsible for shaping the success of Gump's Art Department, offering new and recognized artists alike the opportunity to display their works and inviting the public to appreciate—and purchase—them.

GALLERY DAYS

"During most of the thirty-four years I have worked for Gump's it has seemed more like a labor of love than a job. I never felt each morning as I was preparing to go to the store that I was going to work. It was like I was going to have fun, mainly because of the chance to work with artists and dealers and the works themselves. I felt as if this was my way of contributing something to the community and its intellectual content.

It amazes me, when I look back over the years, how far ahead of the times we were. One of our best shows ever

OPPOSITE PAGE: CAROL FREMLIN'S PAINTING
EXHIBITED IN THE GALLERY ENHANCES THIS
DISPLAY OF PILLOWS MADE FROM ANTIQUE FAB-
RICS, SOME OF THEM WOVEN CENTURIES AGO.
JUST IMAGINE THESE TAPESTRIES, VICTORIAN
NEEDLEPOINTS, AND FLEMISH FABRICS HANGING
AT THE WINDOWS OF AN 18TH CENTURY HOME
OR AS THE LITURGICAL VESTMENTS OF A HIGH
CLERGYMAN.

was "American Folk Art," which was done in the 1960s. It was something very new to the West, and we did it nearly twenty years before it really became popular and a long time before people were educated about it. As one can imagine, prices on the works we have shown over the years are today outrageous. Over the years, one could have seen and bought, quite reasonably, works by Picasso, Henry Moore, Barbara Hepworth, Ben Shahn, John Marin, Morris Graves, and others.

Our new Gump's Gallery, Volume II features more pottery, hand-blown glass, paper constructions, and other objects. This is nothing new for Gump's—we've always had these kinds of works, perhaps not in such quantity or so well publicized. The first show of this work was in 1955 when we introduced Peter Voulkos, John Mason, Robert Arneson, and others.

Today, artisans in hand-blown glass include William Morris, Dante Marioni, Benjamin Moore, Flora Mace, and Joey Kirkpatrick. Pottery pieces are fashioned by Rick Dillingham, David Gilhooly, Rose Cabat, James Crawford, and Ward Kerr. June Schwarcz enamels, Native American Indian arts, and limited editions of illustrated books by Alan James Robinson can be found here with Joel Hoyer's fetish baskets. Each year, the new talents of artisans from all over the country are added to the Gallery display.

HELEN HENINGER

AN INTERVIEW WITH HELEN HENINGER

Heninger's perfect eye has taken in countless works of art in cities in the United States and abroad. Her genuine love of art is to be expected, but her respect for artists is a rare thing in the great wide world of art. Primarily self-taught, she has ferreted out the talents of the obscure, elevating their status from unknown to outstandingly popular. Hired in 1949, while rather nonchalantly looking for work, her days at Gump's began in the China Department. In 1954, she took a six-month leave in order to travel through Europe, at a time when few Americans did so. When she returned to the store, she found her proper niche as an assistant in the Gallery. The die had been cast.

Q: What were the early days in the Gallery like for you?
When I started in the Gallery, I was doing the job I had always wanted. When I was in Europe, I visited every museum and saw every picture. I memorized everything. When I returned, Gump's was kind enough to pick up the tab for any extra schooling that I requested. I had the unique opportunity to meet the artists and set up the shows, which was the nitty-gritty work I really loved.

Q: What was the art scene like in the 1950s in San Francisco?
I went to every opening and visited every artist's studio. It was just a fairy tale way to get going. I had a great job and the contemporary art scene was just beginning.

Q: Whose works did you show?
We showed a lot of new artists who got their starts here. We would show works of students from California College of Arts and Crafts and UC Davis in the art bins so people could start their collections. Nathan Oliveira was teaching and

so was Diebenkorn, at the time. Bryan Wilson was a very big painter and Sam Richardson was a very fine sculptor. There was a whole group of people who are now huge successes.

Q: How did you find new works of art?
People would send me slides, but finding talented people generally meant going and digging them out. It was a wonderful experience to travel, and word of mouth is probably the best way to find someone. I would find myself in someone's studio or out in the country, looking at art.

Q: Does it matter to you whether an artist has a "name " or not?
No, not at all. Very often the people we have shown at the beginnings of their careers have not had major exposure. It was fun to watch their art develop.

Q: Do you think that you participated in the tradition of showing great art at Gump's?
I continued that tradition. We already carried paintings and sculpture, and later we got into pottery and crafts. It was a lot more than just finding new pieces to hang up every month. I would bring in new objects and undiscovered art works as well.

Q: Of all the shows and special exhibitions, of which ones are you most proud?
Besides "American Folk Art" I am especially proud of the English watercolor show, "Fabled Lands," and "The Art of Latin America." That was fabulous.

Q: What made you decide to do the Latin American show?
I just got it into my head that I wanted to do it. And I did it. A lot of artists simply didn't have the recognition they deserved. It was just time to do it.

Q: How did you manage everything—the trips to Europe, the travels within the United States, making contacts everywhere?
I honestly don't know. The only way I was able to handle it was that I didn't have to do intense paperwork and I was able to spend more of my time doing the creative work. I was busy all the time. I would have gotten bored if I couldn't have done something creative. I was always cooking up something new to do.

Q: What has been the most exciting aspect of your work at Gump's through the years?
The doing of it. That's what's most exciting. I love visiting the artists, the one-on-one with them. My juices can get going so much that I can get a headache. After it's all put together and done, I've already had my excitement working with the people involved.

Q: Do you collect anything specific?
I don't any more. I used to. But I think being surrounded by all the art here I haven't found that to be necessary. I have some nice drawings and things in my home. My favorites are works on paper, but they don't have to be by someone famous.

Q: How did it happen that Richard Gump hired you as director of the Gallery?
He was a very surprising man. When I was made director, it happened very fast. In a day. He walked into the Gallery and I asked him, "Who do you think you will make director of the Gallery?" and he said, "You." Then he turned around and walked away. It not only stunned me, I couldn't have been more pleased. He gave me great confidence.

JANET LYNN ROSEMAN

GIRL IN BLUE APRON, OIL ON PANEL BY ROBERT HENRI. ACQUIRED FROM GUMP'S IN 1988, NOW IN THE COLLECTION OF NAN TUCKER McEVOY.

THE FUJITA SHOW

Richard Gump was involved with arranging quite a number of exhibitions in the Gallery. A devoted painter himself, he was dedicated to improving his own artistic style and took evening art classes several times a week. After a wildly successful show of nudes by the Japanese artist Fujita, Richard thought he and his fellow hobbyist painters would greatly benefit if they could learn to adopt Fujita's style. He persuaded Sadie, the art school model, to pose nude for the class one quiet evening in the Gallery after the close of the business day. While the group sketched, they had an unexpected visitor—the night watchman. Unruffled, Richard explained later that they hadn't meant to shock him, only to learn Fujita's style, which, Richard determined, he did.

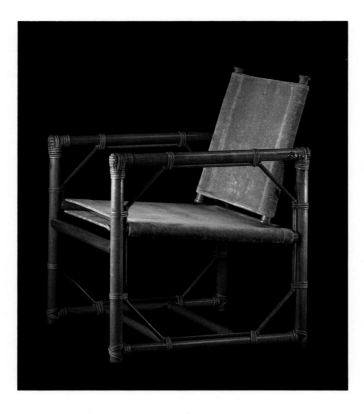

ELEANOR FORBES

"My greatest joy is working with people. I could never be an art-for-art's-sake designer working in isola-tion in my own studio. Designing for modern homes keeps me in touch with craftsmen, with clients who bring their individual furnishing problems to be solved, with architects and fellow designers in various fields. No wonder I am as enthusiastic about my work as the day I started."

E.F.

Eleanor Forbes was "the first lady of interior design" at Gump's for nearly fifty years. Until her retirement in 1972, she was responsible for producing an extraordinary range of custom furniture, accessories, rugs, lighting, and even jewelry for the store's customers. She was the only person ever to receive both Honorary and Lifetime mem-berships in the American Society of Interior Designers.

Although her love of the Orient may have at times bordered on the obsessive, her overall streamlined approach to design was an artistic marriage of simplicity and function. The rattan officer's chair she designed in 1948 is con-sidered a classic and is part of the collection of outstanding contemporary design at the Museum of Modern Art in New York.

A graduate of the California School of the Fine Arts (now called the San Francisco Art Institute), Forbes made a practice of always breaking the rules. Everything about her was striking, including her personal appearance. She dressed in earth tones that were blended and understated but somehow gave her a lot of pizzazz. Her strong will, sin-gularity of purpose, and individuality manifested themselves early. Despite some objection, when she was a high school student she enrolled in several manual training classes and learned to make wood furniture. "We had to go to the lumber room and choose our raw lumber. We'd plane it and cut it. We made our drawings and followed through."

She was hired by Gump's when Henry Judson Allen was the head of the Design Studio. "I did whatever was asked of me. For several years, I designed anything they requested, often sketching furniture ideas to show the client." She also worked with Ben Davis in the Interior Design Department, creating new designs in a selection of

THE OFFICER'S CHAIR AND OTHER "RAWHIDE AND RATTAN" PIECES DESIGNED BY ELEANOR FORBES BECAME POPULAR CLASSICS.

ABOVE: IN THIS SETTING FOR A SMALL DINING ROOM OR DEN, MISS FORBES DEMONSTRATED HER ABILITY TO COUPLE EXACTNESS WITH BEAUTY IN ALL OF HER CUSTOM DESIGN WORK.

OPPOSITE PAGE: THE GREEKS AND ROMANS STORED THEIR VALUABLES IN WOODEN BOXES MUCH LIKE THESE ELABORATELY CARVED AND INLAID CONTAINERS. WHETHER HER BOX HELD LETTERS FROM A COURTESAN TO HER LOVER, FADING PHOTOGRAPHS, OR THE PERSONAL DIARIES OF AN EMPEROR'S MISTRESS, WITH KEY IN HAND THE OWNER KNEW THAT HER SECRETS WERE PROTECTED FROM UNINVITED EYES. IN JAPAN, ROUND BOXES AND SQUARE BOXES, BOXES THAT STAND UP, LIE DOWN, TWIST, AND FOLD ARE AS BEAUTIFUL AS THEY ARE FUNCTIONAL. THE BOXES PICTURED ARE RUSSIAN LACQUERWARE, A KOREAN MEDICINE CHEST, CHINESE IVORY, JAPANESE NESTING BOXES, AND PAINTED ITALIAN FRUITWOOD.

materials including metal, porcelain, art glass, and wood. When Davis left the store to start his own furniture company, TAPP, in Chicago, he invited Forbes to help him introduce a line of furniture with Chinese motifs. This furniture helped earn Eleanor her international reputation. Forbes also worked closely with furniture manufacturers John and Elinor McGuire, who still offer her rattan and rawhide designs in their catalogue.

In addition to prodigious design talents, Forbes was also responsible for the integration of design for all the store's departments. The Design Studio was where she created custom furniture designs, office environments for corporations, and the interiors of homes for the rich and famous. Her method of combining harmonizing elements, a Forbes trademark, made her one of the most recognized designers in the world. "The Design Studio was a new thing for Gump's. We had people who were enthusiastic, who had ideas and the authority in the store to carry them out. We did a lot of creative work. No one else was doing what Gump's was doing in the twenties, thirties, and forties. I wasn't the only one—I suppose I just sort of lasted the longest. I never worked anywhere else, except when they loaned me out to TAPP after World War II. And I was never bored for a day."

She was complimented for being an "architect's designer." She could look at a building and realize exactly what and how much interior design was needed, but Ms. Forbes wanted things done exactly the way she saw them. She had such confidence and sureness of purpose that it was obvious there was only one way to do something—hers.

She was, however, marvelous with her individual clients, much to the delight of Gump's management. She never made a client feel that she was imposing her ideas. A master of subtlety, Forbes let her clients believe it was their own taste and background that provided the ideas and direction for the way in which she decorated their houses. There was tremendous cachet in having an Eleanor Forbes-designed home.

In these years after her 1986 death, Eleanor Forbes' strong influence is still apparent and her work survives the test of time. As she would be pleased to know, her wish that "the things we are creating today will be the heirlooms of tomorrow" has come true.

BREAKING THE RULES

Gump's has had an eternal romance with the elusive but captureable treasures of the past and present. The Lamp Department has designed lamp bases from Japanese hat stands, hookahs, and the even more unusual ceremonial horns from Nepal. A traditional item is bound to show up in a completely innovative fashion. At Gump's, Japanese obis are sold as tabletop accents to highlight enormous donburi bowls used for dessert dishes, and Thai altar tables become serving trays. The buyers have a keen eye for a variety of cultures' most unexpected artifacts, and what they bring back from all over the globe instructs us to see these things in a new way. The Gump philosophy of breaking the rules to achieve interesting combinations and juxtapositions of objects and styles in the home has become a characteristically San Franciscan trait.

WHERE ELSE WOULD YOU EXPECT TO FIND AN OLD WORLD WORKSHOP WHERE LAMPS AND SHADES ARE HAND MADE BY A SPECIALLY TRAINED STAFF THAT EXCELS IN A LOST ART? ALTHOUGH RICHARD GUMP NOTED "TOO MANY LAMPS HIDE THEIR LIGHT UNDER BUSHELS OF HORSE HEADS, BALLET DANCERS, PEKINESE, ABORIGINES, CHINESE SPITOONS, GIRAFFES, CARAFES, NUDES, LUMPS OF FLOWERS OR VEGETATION, IN FACT ANYTHING TO WHICH THE BENEFITS OF SCIENCE ENABLE US TO ATTACH A LIGHT," THE LAMP SHOP COMBINES UNUSUAL OBJECTS AND FINE DESIGN TO CREATE BEAUTIFUL LAMPS THAT SHED LIGHT AND TRANSCEND THE TENDENCY TOWARD IL-LUMINATION TO WHICH MR. GUMP ALLUDED.

HANS GRAG WAS A FINE METAL WORKER WHO CREATED THE DISTINCTIVE, SIMPLE YET ELEGANT HAND-HAMMERED BRASS LAMPS SOLD IN THE STORE. HIS EARLY, OLD WORLD TRAINING WAS UNDER THE PATRONAGE OF A WEALTHY GERMANY BARON, BUT HIS ASSOCIATION WITH GUMP'S PERMITTED HIM TO EXERCISE MORE FREEDOM AND INNOVATION IN HIS WORK. FOR MANY YEARS, HIS WORKSHOP IN THE FOOTHILLS OF THE SIERRAS PRODUCED LAMPS AND SCULPTURE EXCLUSIVELY FOR GUMP'S. EACH PIECE IS INDIVIDUALLY CRAFTED, SIGNED, DATED, AND NUMBERED. AFTER HANS DIED, HIS SON NORMAN AND NORMAN'S SON JOHN CONTINUED IN THE ELDER GRAG'S TRADE, AND NOW HANDCRAFT THEIR OWN DESIGNS AS WELL AS THOSE HANS MADE SO POPULAR. THE EXQUISITE METALWORKS HAVE BEEN SHOWN IN NUMEROUS GALLERIES AND MUSEUMS, INCLUDING THE AVERY BRUNDAGE COLLECTION, THE MARYHILL MUSEUM, AND THE ALUMNI COLLECTION AT NORMAN'S ALMA MATER, THE CALIFORNIA COLLEGE OF ARTS AND CRAFTS. THE GRAG LAMPS AND SCULPTURES HAVE BEEN COMMISSIONED BY GOVERNMENT AND PRIVATE CONTRACT, AND ARE INSTALLED IN LIBRARIES, MUNICIPAL BUILDINGS, AND CHURCHES AND SYNAGOGUES THROUGHOUT THE COUNTRY. THE GRAG LAMPS ARE AVAILABLE AT GUMP'S TODAY.

AT YOUR SERVICE

Impeccable service is a Gump's given. When a Beverly Hills celebrity selected a full set of Flora Danica, the most expensive china in the store (a pattern that had been designed especially for Catherine the Great and is probably the most expensive porcelain service in the world), for his wedding day and gave only two day's notice, his order was fulfilled. But the china was not all that he received. On the day of the wedding, the store's manager unwrapped each precious plate by hand.

Regular shoppers become a part of the family whether they visit once a month or once a year. It is not unusual to find three generations of San Franciscans returning to the store year after year to purchase gifts for family and friends, update or commission new jewelry, or find special decorative pieces for their homes.

When Barbra Streisand admired the water lilies in the Beverly Hills store's display she asked where she might buy them, since she couldn't find a florist in town to supply her pond with the fragrant blossoms. The store manager offered to fill her pond with water lilies when he received his next shipment, and he continued this extra service for several months, attention nearly unheard of today.

WATER IS THE IDEAL MEDIUM FOR SHOWING THE SHIMMERING BEAUTY OF BUCCELLATI STERLING SILVER LEAVES.

PRIVACY GUARANTEED

Privacy is understood—completely. Celebrities, royalty, and heads of state like Leontyne Price, the Queen of Spain, and Princess Alexandra of England know they can visit after-hours to do personal shopping without fanfare. "Guilty spouses" who purchase gifts for their respective spouses—or someone else's—know that discretion is always the better part of valor.

ONCE UPON A TIME, SILVER WAS SO SCARCE AND VALUABLE IT WAS CONFISCATED BY ROYALTY TO KEEP TREASURIES SOLVENT, AND SILVERSMITHS HAD TO FIGHT FOR EVERY OUNCE THEY USED. WHEN IT BECAME AVAILABLE TO CRAFTSMEN WITHOUT ROYAL PATRONAGE, EACH DESIGNER HAD HIS OWN HALLMARK STAMPED ON THE SILVER AND GOLD ARTICLES HE WROUGHT. MASTER SILVERSMITHS PAST AND PRESENT ARE REPRESENTED IN THE SILVER ROOM'S COLLECTION.

THE "GRANDUCA," NAPOLEON'S "IVY," AND THE BLACK BIRDS

PREVIOUS SPREAD: A MAJOR TRADITION AT GUMP'S HAS BEEN THE EDIFICATION, AMUSEMENT, AND ENTERTAINMENT OF THE PUBLIC WITH DELIGHTFUL DISPLAYS OF PLACE SETTINGS. NOT ONLY DOES THE STORE SELL PARTICULAR CHINA AND SILVER PATTERNS, IN A VERY DIDACTIC, ALBEIT ROMANTIC WAY, IT TEACHES THE ART OF MIX AND MATCH, BREAKING ALL THE RULES.

ABOVE, LEFT: "GRANDUCA."

ABOVE, RIGHT: BLACK "AVES."

OPPOSITE: THE CHINA FEATURED IN THIS CONTEMPORARY ADVERTISEMENT IS CLOISONNÉ BY ROYAL CROWN DERBY, INSPIRED BY ANTIQUE ORIENTAL CLOISONNÉ.

While searching in Italy for special collections to highlight the 1989 special promotion "A Tribute to Italy," the Gump's contingent visited the Doccia Museum outside Florence. Within its walls, we found a remarkably fresh and beautiful floral pattern created by Marquis Carlo Ginori when porcelain production in Europe was just beginning. "Granduca," as the pattern is called, was produced between 1745 and 1750. It had been unseen for more than two hundred years, except by visitors to the Doccia.

Ginori, the original manufacturer of the pattern, who still produces porcelain of the highest quality, agreed to an unprecedented request and brought "Granduca" back to life in a complete dinner service. It was Ginori's contribution to "A Tribute to Italy," and Gump's was doubly honored—Richard Ginori made the service and it was offered exclusively for one year. It has since become a popular international best-seller.

When Napoleon was exiled to the island of Elba, the British who were responsible for his comfort while in captivity presented him with a special china dinner service. Its design, a somewhat claustrophobic tangle of ivy vines, symbolized the deposed emperor's status—he was as bound to the island as the ivy to the plate. In honor of Gump's 1985 "British Style" exhibition, the original manufacturer, Wedgwood, recreated the pattern in bone china. At the same time, Gump's also requested china manufacturers Royal Doulton to make one of their more popular patterns, "Aves," available in a distinctive black and white. The reception of that pattern at Gump's led to its introduction and subsequent success internationally.

WILLIAM GOULET

The Great Wall of China at Gump's is an array of hundreds upon hundreds of patterns of fine china. Patrons are encouraged to select pieces that appeal to them and combine china patterns with flatware and linen to create a fully appointed table. Fortunately, the Fates protected this grand display during the 1989 San Francisco earthquake, when not a single dish, bowl, or cup was broken.

VISITING CHINA: TABLES OF CONTENT

Times change. Tastes take many turns. When I married in London nineteen years ago, I set aside some romantic dreams for the moment and decided to be seventies-practical about dinnerware. My fiance and I chose Ceralene's pure white "Marly" dinnerware, a pristine Empire design, with generous dinner plates and beautifully proportioned cups.

I really wanted Ceralene's colorful "Vieux Chine," a vibrant chinoiserie pattern that had originally been designed for the Compagnie Française des Indes at the request of the Marquis de Pompadour. In Paris I'd discovered "Houqua," another unusual made-in-Limoges design inspired by a rare Kang-Hi period painting, with the earth, sun, and moon orbiting an earthly paradise. White won out.

We set up our first apartment in Georgetown, and "Marly" became the background of many wonderful dinner parties.

Over the years I've added Bernardaud's gold-banded white "Pacaudiere" dinner plates and Annieglass's platinum-banded glass plates to my table repertoire, along with a few pieces of "Laurier Blue."

Lately, I'm in a new dinnerware buying mood and I've been haunting Gump's. I'm not matching sets anymore, but for new plates I'm eyeing "Vieux Chine" and "Houqua" again. They're timeless, and would look perfect in my all-white San Francisco apartment. And I love Puiforcat's "Galluchat Green" with its gold-banded shagreen border. Plain celadon looks rather chic. Hand-painted pottery plates feel right, too.

Then I discovered Herend's knock-out dinner plates with their very-this-minute poison-green basket-weave borders outlined in elegant matte gold. They remind me of Lacroix ballgowns, springtime in Paris, "Mitsouko" perfume, old roses. Romance and the unexpected meet head-on. I think maybe this is the way I want to spend the nineties.

DIANE DORRANS SAEKS

ABOVE: T. S. ELIOT WROTE POETRY WITH IMAGES OF LIFE MEASURED OUT IN COFFEE SPOONS AND LAUGHTER TINKLING AMONG THE TEACUPS. AT GUMP'S THERE ARE MILES OF TEACUPS AND ROW UPON ROW OF SILVER SPOONS FROM WHICH TO ENJOYABLY MEASURE ONE'S LIFE.

OPPOSITE: IN THIS RECENT ADVERTISEMENT, GUMP'S CONTINUES AS AN INTERNATIONAL TREASURE TROVE: THE BLACK GLASS SERVICE PLATE IS MADE IN AMERICA BY VIKING; THE SILVER, TALISMAN NOIR BY CHRISTOFLE IS DECORATED BY REAL CHINESE LACQUER; THE DINNERWARE, MARLY BY CERALENE, IS FRENCH.

TASTE

THE AMBIANCE OF GUMP'S IS TASTE. THE TASTE of the Orient. The taste of Europe. The taste of San Francisco. The atmosphere is inviting, attractive, and tempting. Gump's highlights the special, the personal, and the distinct. It comprises the familiar and the foreign, the formal and the casual, the fragile and the durable, the "priceless" and the affordable, the mundane and the exotic. And, above all, the unexpected.

The experience of Gump's is the impression one takes away, as Henry James said in 1888 in *The Art of Fiction*.

"The power to guess the unseen from the seen, to trace the implications of things, to judge the whole piece by the pattern, the condition of feeling life in general so completely that you are well on your way to knowing any particular corner of it—this cluster of gifts may almost be said to constitute experience....If experience consists of impressions, it may be said that impressions are experience."

SAN FRANCISCO STYLE
A TOUR OF SAN FRANCISCO HOUSES

On sycamore-shaded Pacific Avenue, a 1903 Bernard Maybeck shingled house opens its black-framed windows to the deep green cypresses of the Presidio. The graceful Maybeck-designed lotus-shaped copper drainpipe, now ennobled with verdigris, is reported to have cost the original owners more than the house.

Atop Russian Hill, an art collector's villa turns its back to the view, preferring instead the inspiration of bold paintings by Bay Area figurative artists. Nearby, a chic white modernist house designed by an assistant to Joseph Strauss, chief engineer of the Golden Gate Bridge, gazes down on the quiet Bay as fog drifts over the headlands. Along Francisco Street, creamy-pink "Penelope" roses tumble over a white pergola.

Near Lafayette Park, a noble columned mansion built with a sugar baron's fortune is decorated with intricate flowers, Della Robbia garlands and putti, as sweet as icing on a wedding cake.

Along California Street, a trio of turn-of-the-century Victorians primp in the sunshine, gaily painted ornamentation belying the fast approach of their centennial.

On the grande luxe end of Broadway, houses in a Grand Tour of international styles from gothic to Tudor to Bauhaus to palazzo stand on solid bedrock with private-box views of the romantic Palace of Fine Arts.

Surrounded by a garden of luscious white rhododendrons in a quiet corner of Russian Hill, a landmark shingled Willis Polk house is now a very private showcase of international art.

Tremors and temblors come and go, but San Franciscans continue to cling to their hills, and to a heightened sense of good fortune. From Telegraph Hill to glamorous Nob Hill and Pacific Heights and beyond to Seacliff, this is their territory. Nothing can shake San Franciscans' long-held belief that they are living in the best possible city. A hint of superiority is apparent, with absolutely no apologies.

Their unwavering confidence, of course, comes naturally. Frequent travel only heightens their appreciation of San Francisco's riches. This world is a rather privileged one where the season is always spring, the sunny setting has not changed dramatically in fifty years, and rooms are filled with treasures gathered all over the map.

They guard their privacy, these city dwellers. Windows are oriented to remarkable Bay views, to well-tended green-on-green private gardens, never the street. The observant passerby may catch glimpses through a window of fringed tussah silk draperies or slightly faded chintz curtains, stylishly rolled tortoiseshell bamboo shades, a fragment of an Imari plate or celadon bowl, or the corner of a bold oil painting, clues to the lives within.

In a Vallejo Street house, garden roses fill a Baccarat vase, and a well-worn book on jade is placed at the ready beside a comfortable down-filled chair lit by northern light. An unpretentious canvas-upholstered sofa stands in an updated Victorian house as a counterpoint to an elaborate Chinese lacquered chest, and a Biedermeier secretaire.

Cable cars clatter and clang along bustling streets. Inside the houses of San Francisco, it's another story.

San Franciscans dress their houses to please themselves, paying little attention to fast-changing fads. They have never intended their rooms to be this-minute shiny new, or made the social faux pas of imagining that their houses might serve as character references and thus speed their way up the social ladder.

These well-proportioned rooms reflect worldliness and a taste for timeless design, not a desire to impress. Decoration for the sake of flaunting wealth is not the point.

With overstuffed chairs and sofas, old carpets with character, contemporary paintings, piles of books and magazines, family photos in silver frames, simply arranged flowers, and glasses of chilled mineral water at hand, these rooms encourage a sense of well-being, undisturbed by the outside world. They welcome with open arms after a summer at Lake Tahoe, and offer a refuge during the round of opera opening-night parties, symphony concerts, and ballet balls.

At home, city style-setters fearlessly cross borders of the imagination, mixing furniture and decorative objects of several periods and countries at whim.

PREVIOUS SPREAD: "A CROWD OF CRYSTAL CHAMPAGNE FLUTES PROMISES AN EVENING OF ENCHANTMENT TO ALL WHO TASTE THE NECTAR OF THE GODS. THE SUPPER, DURING WHICH THE GUESTS BEHAVED LIKE CHILDREN, CONSISTED LARGELY OF CHAMPAGNE WITH A FEW THINGS THROWN IN LIKE BOUILLON, TRUFFLES, AND DUCK. THERE WAS NO STINT IN THE CHAMPAGNE LIKE THE USUAL STINGY ONE QUART TO A PERSON AT MOST NEW YORK BALLS. SEE HOW IT PUNS AND QUIBBLES IN THE GLASS."

LUCIUS BEEBE
THE BIG SPENDERS

LEFT: THIS 19TH CENTURY CHINESE ANCESTRAL PORTRAIT IS INDEED AN IMPOSING FIGURE OF AUTHORITY, AND ONE THAT A. L. GUMP WOULD HAVE LIKED. HIS YOUTHFUL EXCURSIONS INTO CHINATOWN'S QUAINT OLD CURIO SHOPS INTRODUCED HIM TO THE MYTHS AND TALES OF CHINA. AT THAT TIME, IN THE 1870S, EXCEPT FOR THE CANTONESE MERCHANTS, NO ONE IN SAN FRANCISCO IMPORTED CHINESE WARES. LATER, AT THE HELM OF THE STORE, HE WAS TAUGHT THE DETAILS OF CHINESE ART AND HISTORY BY THE WELL-TRAVELLED ED NEWELL, GUMP'S' BUYER FOR ORIENTAL MERCHANDISE. FORTUNATELY, A. L. BECAME A WALKING COMPENDIUM OF FACTS ABOUT CHINESE ART, FOR AT THAT TIME THERE WERE NO BOOKS ON THE SUBJECT AVAILABLE IN ENGLISH.

International scope and an enlightened world view have always been signatures of San Francisco designers. Thanks to decades of informed travel—or to decorative arts stores and galleries that shop for them—San Franciscans have been able to choose from the best the world has to offer. They have the wit and the imagination to see the affinity between China Trade porcelains and Chippendale chairs, handsome old tansus and contemporary rattan furniture, made-in-California handcrafts and the finest French crystal, an Imari bowl and well-worn Killim rugs. Editing and art directing rooms are second nature.

From San Francisco interior design gurus like Michael Taylor and Eleanor Ford, Anthony Hall and John Dickinson, they have learned well.

Furniture of the late 18th Century is a particular favorite of interior designer Anthony Hall. In his own Russian Hill house he lives with late Louis Seize fauteils, Chinese lacquer tables, a Russian chandelier, Italian fabrics, and a lifelong collection of architectural drawings. He has noted, however, that few of his clients today would want a roomful of fine antiques. Instead, they'll start with family heirlooms and fill in with top-quality reproductions and contemporary classics.

As designer John Dickinson has said, the best design is not all de luxe. San Franciscans love to find (and receive) elegant silverware, French porcelain, antique bibelots, hand-detailed antique chests, but a scheme that's all correct proportions and perfection can be ultimately rather stiff, not welcoming. It must have lightness, a little eccentricity, to temper the gilt-edged design.

Designer Scott Lamb's search for quality of design translates to subtle rooms with French, American, and English antiques, Japanese lacquered tables, Chinese porcelains—the best he can find—given an edge with a quirky chintz upholstered chair or pillows, beautiful but inexpensive objects on a table. A tour of his rooms is a glimpse of his passions, his sense of humor.

Ultimately, houses in San Francisco express a remarkable individuality. No one style, no one look predominates. Northern California's light points up the details, the differences.

To walk into hospitable rooms, to stand at a window to catch the last burnished rays of sunset over the Golden Gate Bridge, is to experience the private face of San Francisco.

Clearly, these houses, these rooms, could never exist anywhere else.

DIANE DORRANS SAEKS

A TASTE OF EVERYTHING

All of one's senses are delighted by a visit to Gump's. Attention to detail is a top priority, and nothing is overlooked. There are fresh floral arrangements, which fill the air with the fragrance of exotic lilies; cool jade carvings and antique silk damasks to handle; a gallery exhibiting the work of outstanding American artists; custom-designed divans and armchairs in which to sink luxuriously; thick carpets and fine tiles underfoot. Clearly, a taste of everything and everything in good taste, whether it be the visual or tactile, contemporary or antique.

THE HOUSE IN GOOD TASTE

The early Victorians believed their furnishings would last through their lifetimes and often chose the most expensive materials and finishes, ranging from inlaid gilt and gold mirrors to cut crystal glassware. Over the next one hundred years, styles changed radically from roccoco to art deco to art nouveau, modernism, and the functional streamlined approach of today. Although taste changes from decade to decade, our homes are still a reflection of taste, and probably good taste at that.

Elsie De Wolfe, the first lady of interior design, wrote in *The House in Good Taste* in 1913:

"A house is a dead giveaway....We are sure to judge a woman in whose house we find ourselves for the first time, by her surroundings. We judge her temperament, her habits, her inclinations, by the interior of her home. We may talk of the weather, but we are looking at the furniture."

THIS INVITING SAN FRANCISCO-STYLE MODEL LIVING ROOM HAS BEEN CREATED BY THE GUMP'S INTERIOR DESIGN DEPARTMENT. LOCATED ON THE THIRD FLOOR OF THE STORE, IT CREATES NEW INTERIORS FOR IN-STORE ENVIRONMENTS AS WELL AS PATRONS' OWN HOMES ON AN EVER-CHANGING BASIS.

SIXTY YEARS OF INTERIOR DESIGN
The World of McMillen

Erica Brown

Viking · SIXTY YEARS OF INTERIOR DESIGN · Preface by Albert Hadley

RICHARD GUMP'S AXIOMS OF GOOD TASTE

1. Age is not an automatic measure of value.
2. A work of art is a work of art in any material.
3. An out-of-the-ordinary method of manufacture is not a guarantee of extraordinary value.
4. A foreign stamp is no criterion for extra value.
5. Costliness does not necessarily assure comeliness.
6. A master does not always create a masterpiece.
7. The relics of the renowned aren't always desirable.
8. Overelaboration is not beauty.
9. The latest thing is not the best thing per se.
10. It is crazy to try to live beyond your means—financially, culturally, or physically.
11. Emotional reactions, personal prejudices, and predilections do not point the way; to reach the right destination it is necessary to understand and appreciate the basic demands of good design.
12. There are worthwhile things and many worthless things on the market.

RICHARD GUMP AND THE GOOD TASTE TEST

Richard Gump was a man with the habit of passion: passion for art, for music, for culture, for life itself. A true Renaissance man, he not only did things well, he did them with style. Performer, composer, painter, furniture designer, perpetual scholar, bon vivant, and merchant prince—Richard's accomplishments are impressive. He had the opportunity, the means, and the style to indulge in a dilettante's dream of culture and the arts. An exemplary zeal for the good things in life enabled him to focus on his various quests with an almost impenetrable intensity. He seized the challenge of educating the public about "good taste" with a fervor more appropriate to a missionary, but, upon further reflection, one has to admit that it was very much *his* mission.

He lived and breathed good taste practically from the cradle. Travelling far and wide as a child with his mother, from one suite of grande luxe rooms to another, and growing up in the store as well instilled in him a desire for flamboyant behavior and the best to be had in this life. His was scarcely the stuff of a conventional upbringing. Obsessed with the cultivation of knowledge, and blessed with the rare ability to mentally catalogue information, Gump developed a memory of amazing breadth and ease. Friends and staff who travelled with him agree that he was well versed on just about any subject, and that his encyclopedic mind was not only intimidating, it was astonishing. His close associate and companion Johanna Sianta regarded him as "one of the great teachers of culture in all its forms. Without lecturing or pontificating, he imparts knowledge in a very natural and easy way which makes art, architecture, music, and history a daily pleasure…a rare trait in one who knows so much."

His philosophy of retailing included the belief that customers, no matter what their economic strata, welcomed guidance in the selection of merchandise. In his more than three hundred public appearances and his book *Good Taste Costs No More* published by Doubleday in 1951, supporting his one-man crusade for tastefulness, he succeeded in persuading the public that "not only is it better to buy the best, but it is often the best buy."

Gump took the issue of good taste to the very heart of the store's operations, going so far in 1952 as to devise the now infamous Good Taste Test. Looking at 137 illustrations of classic furniture, room arrangements, table settings, sculptures, candelabra, silver flatware, crystal stemware, and individual examples of a range of historic styles, every prospective store employee had to determine whether the designs were of good or bad taste. Gump wanted to preselect salespeople of lofty taste standards to give the store the tone he believed appropriately befitted it. No one was exempt from this test—it mattered not if they were going to work in the basement or in the Baccarat salon. The answers were weighed against the decisions of a national group of design experts with Gump at the helm. The test was used as a barometer for an inclination toward good taste. Gump wanted the staff to have a "feel for taste" as much as a feel for merchandising.

The results of each employee's test were reported only to Gump, his secretary Mrs. Graham, and the director of personnel, so the staff would be disinclined to compare the scores of their "tasteful" abilities. While there is no question that such a test would be controversial today, even then it was surprising. Some employees objected to being required to take the test, but for others it provided the proverbial golden opportunity. When the personnel director brought one man's high score to Mr. Gump's attention, the man was invited to meet him. Gump offered him the chance to leave his position as a gift wrapper, and he later became a buyer for the Oriental Department.

Some people found Richard Gump brash, but he could be charming. His niece Marilyn called him "a gregarious recluse." "He had a built-in style detector and he could clearly tell if someone had *it* or not." A bit of an autocrat, he maintained that if " 'you gotta ask,' you either haven't got good taste or you don't know you have." He took the matter of good taste very seriously. When Richard died in 1989, it signalled the end of an especially colorful era in Gump's history.

JANET LYNN ROSEMAN

RICHARD GUMP'S MUSIC: FROM CLASSICAL TO OOM-PAH

When Richard was the president of the store, he hosted a two-hour classical music program on a local radio station every Thursday evening. He thought of himself as possibly the first classical music disc jockey, and sponsored the show with no commercial interruptions.

He also dreamed up the Guckenheimer Sour Kraut Band, a group humorously modelled after the Bavarian bands that performed in prewar Berlin clubs and bierstubes. "We didn't have exact tempos and we'd sound like a high school orchestra playing a third-rate football team." The nine-piece band performed at grand openings, art and garden fairs, wine celebrations, Oktoberfests, and charity events. The ill-fitting pseudomilitary costumes were as outrageous as the sound of the band, whose particular brand of "oom-pah" was an acquired taste. The band recorded three albums and appeared on a few popular television programs.

Gump was actually a serious performer and composer who had studied piano, violin, and cello with the best teachers in San Francisco. He became more alive when in the company of musicians and music lovers and he was not modest about his special gifts. "Everything I wrote, I wrote because I understand music. I didn't just do it by ear, I knew what made a thing sound German, Italian, or South Seas. Whatever it was, I knew the reason for it sounding that way." Many compositions were performed during his lifetime, and he made numerous recordings.

THE PHILANTHROPISTS

San Francisco residents have long enjoyed the largesse of Gump's, perhaps even unknowingly. The store and its own-ers have always played an active role in charitable organizations and community concerns. The War Memorial Opera House is home to two fine Gobelin tapestries, donated by A. L. Gump, formerly owned by Ferdinand, whose death at Sarajevo precipitated World War I. Companion tapestries hang in the Metropolitan Museum.

Civic contributions of funds, the proceeds of auctions of rare art, and gifts of china, porcelain, and glassware have been regularly presented to local charities and organizations, including the Edgewood Children's Center and the San Francisco ASPCA. Gump's has a tradition of actively contributing to the San Francisco Opera, Symphony, and Museum of Modern Art.

When Gump's sponsors the unique in-store exhibitions, much to the delight of San Francisco's citizenry, opening night traditionally benefits various charities and cultural organizations. In October 1990, Gump's hosted a benefit for the "Light Up the Palace of Fine Arts" campaign to provide permanent lighting for the much-heralded landmark. Nor have the store's efforts gone unnoticed. Elizabeth Taylor visited the Beverly Hills store personally to thank the man-agement for its contribution of outstanding tabletop displays for her Designer Showcase held to raise money for AIDS research.

Museums have long been the beneficiaries of Gump family philanthropy. The San Francisco Museum of Modern Art received a James Kelly painting and the de Young Museum now houses a portrait of John Tait of Harveston by Sir Henry Raeburn, originally shown at the Raeburn Exhibition in Edinburgh in 1876. At his death, Richard Gump bequeathed the one million dollar "Madonna and Child" by Jacobo dell Sellaio (pictured below) as well. The bulk of his estate will be divided among the cultural institutions of San Francisco. Richard Gump's contributions to the Asian Art Museum were acknowledged in the 1980s when a wing was named in his honor.

OPPOSITE: THE GUMP'S BUYERS IN VENICE, 1928. RICHARD LED HIS TEAM THROUGHOUT EUROPE, AND HERE PAUSED BRIEFLY IN ONE OF THEIR FAVORITE CITIES AT THE PIAZZA SAN MARCO. LEFT TO RIGHT: STANLEY CORCORAN; RICHARD GUMP (IN DERBY); RAG. R. "RENZO" BORELLI, GUMP'S AGENT IN ITALY; AND TWO OTHER BUYERS FOR VENETIAN GLASS.

LEFT: THE SITTING ROOM OF THE LATE RICHARD GUMP, SHOWING THE SELLAIO "MADONNA AND CHILD." THE PAINTING WAS LEFT TO THE FINE ARTS MUSEUMS OF SAN FRANCISCO.

GUMPISMS

"Good is not good enough. The best is never too good. Always, when you can, purchase the very finest."

❖

"The way things are done is more eloquent than what they are done with."

❖

"An attractive assembly of good things is the final goal of good taste."

❖

"There is a striking characteristic shared by those with good taste: They are the first to acclaim worthwhile new things. They have not become shortsighted from the habit of appreciating only what they are used to."

❖

"Aesthetic value is within the reach of everyone and should be the paramount consideration in making any purchase, to show, in short, that good taste costs no more."

❖

"We do not know how to judge the merit, desirability, the value of things....We lose sight of one simple consideration without which everything else is meaningless. Is it good looking? Is it beautiful, is it well designed, does it delight the eye?"

Two tasteful ladies in the store's Oriental Department, c. 1930.

"TO GUMP IT"

Emily Post gives an accurate account of a motor trip she took in 1915 from coast to coast. The author tells of the difficulties encountered, the pleasures, the interesting people and places, with all the charm and grace of a romance. The chapter on San Francisco is delightfully entertaining and includes the following:

In San Francisco we rushed early each morning to the [Panama-Pacific International] Exposition and spent no time anywhere else. Every now and then someone said to Pauline, with whom we were stopping, the mysterious sentence: "Have you taken them to Gump's?" And her answer: "Why no, I haven't," was always uttered in that abashed apologetic tone that acknowledges a culpable forgetfulness. Finally one day instead of driving out towards the Exposition grounds we turned towards the heart of the city.

"Where are we going?" I asked.

"To Gump's!" triumphantly.

"To Gump's? Of all the queer sounding things, what is to Gump's?"

"Our most celebrated shop. You must not leave San Francisco without seeing their Japanese and Chinese things."

Shades of dullness, thought I, as if there were not shops enough in New York! As for Oriental treasures, I was sure there were more on Fifth Avenue than are left in Asia. But Pauline being determined, there was nothing for us to do but, as E. M. said, "to Gump it!"

In this museum-shop the room devoted to jades and primitives has night-blue walls overlaid with gold lacquer lattices and brass carvings, and in it the most wonderful treasures of all. They are kept hidden away in silk-lined boxes, and are brought out and shown to you, Chinese fashion, one at a time, so that none shall detract from the other. In one of the Japanese rooms there were decorated paper walls held up by light bamboo frames, amber paper *shoji* instead of windows, and the floors covered with *tatami,* the Japanese floor mats, two inches thick. You sit on the floor as in Japan and drink tea, while silks of every variety are brought to you.

We were told that a rather famous collector went out to see the Fair. On his first day in San Francisco—he was stopping at the St. Francis Hotel which is only a stone's throw across the square—he went idly into this most alluring of shops and became so interested he stayed all day. The next day he did the same, and the third morning found him there again. Finally he said with a sigh: "Having come to see the Exposition, I *must* go out there this afternoon and look at it, as I have to go back to New York tomorrow."

EMILY POST
By Motor to the Golden Gate

GUMPISMS

"Who are the arbiters of taste? Designers and decorators, the good ones, are the primary arbiters of taste, and although their approaches differ and their conclusions vary…they have learned to appraise and accept good things and discard phonies. But there is no definite set of rules evolved out of their experience for us to follow."

❖

"Public notice of a new design starts a fad; when public acceptance is enthusiastic it becomes a style, and when it is accepted generally, it becomes fashion. Wonderful and peculiar things derive from this constant necessity for change."

❖

"Fashions have a recurring cycle of popularity, reminding us that we cannot escape or evade the past. Some fashions of years gone by serve us well, but others are out of place and step today."

❖

"There are many times when knowing the price will suggest a fair idea of value. But in the field of aesthetics, it's a pretty shaky indicator."

❖

"Besides our own peculiar preferences, there are many basic desires shared by all of us that influence our habits and habitats."

"Ah…Gump's. That hush, plush cloister of impeccable taste. The store that Time magazine called "as aloof as Kipling's cat." The swank emporium with enough mystique to rival Marlene Dietrich.

"When dowagers die, if they've been very, very good, they go to Heaven's version of Gump's. Or at least that's what they pray for. For over 140 years, Gump's has been a bastion of rarefied chic, a pricey holdout in a dress-for-less world.."

MANDY BEHBEHANI
"Behind the Swank Curtain"

LEFT: THE ORIENTAL DEPARTMENT HAS CONTIN-UED TO HONOR A. L. GUMP'S INTENTION TO PRESENT TO THE WORLD EXOTIC AND WONDROUS ARTIFACTS FROM THE ORIENT. THE DEPARTMENT IS LADEN WITH THE UNUSUAL—19TH CENTURY JADE BUCKLES, CINNABAR ELEPHANTS, BRONZE BUDDHAS AND ANTIQUE PORCELAINS, ALL ATTRACTIVELY DISPLAYED WITH ELEGANT SIMPLIC-ITY. THE INNER AND OUTER JADE ROOMS BECKON COLLECTORS TO ENTER A WORLD WHERE THEY CAN SEE CARVED OBJECTS MADE FROM JADE AND AMBER, AND JADE TABLETS THAT PRESERVE THE WRITING OF CHIN LING, EMPEROR OF CHINA. IF THESE TREASURES COULD SPEAK, WHAT TALES THEY WOULD TELL!

OVERLEAF: THE FIRST GLASS BOTTLES WERE CREATED BY THE EGYPTIANS MORE THAN FOUR THOUSAND YEARS AGO WHEN THEY CAREFULLY WOUND THREADS OF MOLTEN GLASS AROUND A CORE OF SCULPTED SAND. THE ANCIENT BOTTLES WERE COSTLY TO PRODUCE AND HELD COSMET-ICS, MEDICINAL OINTMENTS, AND PERFUMES. NO DOUBT CLEOPATRA HERSELF SELECTED SCENTS FROM THE MOST BEAUTIFUL BOTTLES MADE. THE FOLKLORE SURROUNDING PERFUME CONTINUES TODAY. OUR GREATEST ROMANTIC FANTASIES ARE CAPTURED BY THE ALLURE OF SCENT, WHICH PROMISES TO BEWITCH AND BRING LOVE TO ALL WHO ARE WILLING TO BELIEVE IN ITS POWERS.

"Taste. You cannot buy such a rare and wonderful thing. You can't send away for it in a catalogue. And I'm afraid it's becoming obsolete."

ROSALIND RUSSELL

"These questions of taste, of feeling, of inheritance need no settlement. Everyone carries his own inch-rule of taste, and amuses himself by applying it triumphantly wherever he travels."

HENRY ADAMS

"Taste is the only morality.... Tell me what you like and I'll tell you what you are."

JOHN RUSKIN, 1866

"No one ever went broke underestimating the taste of the American people."

Attributed to
H.L. MENCKEN

"Good taste is better than bad taste, but bad taste is better than no taste."

ARNOLD BENNETT

THE FIRST TIME GUMP'S OFFERED CUSTOMERS A PUBLIC VIEWING AND
OPPORTUNITY TO BUY CRYSTAL STEMWARE FROM THE CRISTALLERIES DE
SAINT-LOUIS WAS IN THE 1970S. THE RESPONSE WAS FAVORABLE AND
THE STORE HAS CARRIED SAINT-LOUIS SINCE. THE ORIGIN OF THIS
CRYSTAL IS TRACED TO THE MUSTHAL GLASSWORKS, WHICH BEGAN
OPERATIONS IN 1586. BUT EVEN AS EARLY AS 1469, THE DUKE OF
LORRAINE GRANTED SPECIAL PRIVILEGES TO THE GLASSMAKERS OF THE
REGION FOR THEIR FINE ARTISTRY. SINCE THAT TIME THE TRADITION
HAS BEEN UPHELD BY THE SAME FAMILIES WHO HAVE PASSED TOOLS,
CUSTOMS, AND SKILL FROM ONE GENERATION TO ANOTHER.

THE WINDOWS AT GUMP'S ATTRACT AND ENTERTAIN PASSERS-BY AND SHOPPERS WITH HIGHLY ORIGINAL AND CAPTIVATING DISPLAYS DURING THE HOLIDAY SEASON AND ALL YEAR ROUND.

GUMP'S CHRISTMAS WINDOWS

When I was a child growing up near Cleveland, a trip to the city to see the department store window displays signalled the start of the Christmas season. Each December, my entire family, dressed in their best, would pile into the car to pay a visit to Santa, have a special lunch, shop for gifts, and—most of all—to view downtown Cleveland transformed into a magical Christmas wonderland.

Many years later, and now an adult living in San Francisco, I happily recapture that feeling each Christmas. Walking along Post Street, I join the jostling crowds to catch a glimpse of Gump's windows. And each year, the windows not only meet the high expectations formed by my early memories, they surpass them.

As just another enthralled observer, I am drawn into whatever fantasy the windows evoke: antique mechanical figures from around the world; ethereal, delicate Christmas trees; a theatrical rendition of Dickens' *A Christmas Carol.* As an artist, I recognize a kindred spirit behind the creation of Gump's windows and respect their amazing, inventive artfulness.

It seems clear that the windows derive from someone's personal artistic vision, rather than an impersonal committee. In fact, I suspect that the creator of these displays may be portraying aspects of him- or herself. Perhaps that is the secret to why the windows elicit a strong response and generate widespread acclaim. There is certainly more than just dedication and creativity at work here. With these displays, as with most art that captivates, beneath the surface lie remarkable skill, accomplished technique, clever use of materials—and hours of painstaking labor.

My favorites of recent years include the wonderful Fabergé windows. Picture, if you will, Fabergélike eggs, each four or five feet high, perched on elaborately carved stands. As I watched, each giant egg opened slowly and rhythmically to reveal a precious gift. I also especially enjoyed the Japanese windows, simple yet mysterious, dotted with jewellike figures and sculptural shapes. And then there was the popular series of windows showcasing homeless, adoptable pets from the ASPCA. I imagine that these live, cuddly animals, who always looked perfectly comfortable in their whimsical surroundings, took a lot of frantic behind-the-scenes care.

I feel lucky in many ways to live in San Francisco, a place where everyday reality is made beautiful by its natural setting. Most of all, I'm grateful that a half-mile stroll from my South of Market studio can set me in the midst of a dream—elegant and ephemeral—a gift to us, all children, at Christmas.

GARY BUKOVNIK

Gary Bukovnik is a San Francisco painter of watercolors. One of his paintings has become an Aubusson tapestry.

S.P.C.A. Holiday Adoption Cruise

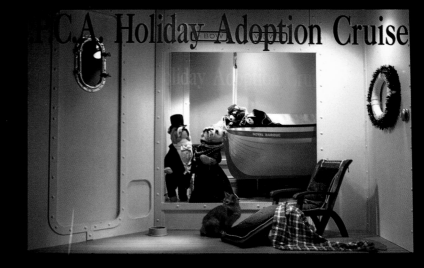

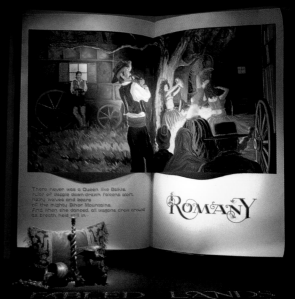

IN AND OUT THE WINDOWS
AN INTERVIEW WITH BOB MAHONEY

Robert J. Mahoney, the doyen of design wizardry at Gump's, has been the mastermind behind the fabulous window and store displays for the past thirty years. As display director, Mahoney is often asked to create the impossible, the untried, the unknown, and has succeeded on all fronts. His ability to transform window displays into "high art" has earned him awards and citations from his peers, including induction into the National Association of Display Industries' Hall of Fame, and The Fashion Institute of San Francisco has created the Robert Mahoney award, which is presented to outstanding students of visual merchandising.

In the late 1950s, Mahoney began working on the Gump's Christmas windows while he was technical director for the Actors' Workshop. He credits his time at the Actors' Workshop with teaching him to "see." By 1961, he was working full-time on the store's windows. His artistry, imagination, attention to detail, and nurturance of perfection are evident in each and every display.

Q: How did you get connected with Gump's originally?
One of the designers at the Actors' Workshop was working at Gump's and I called him to see if there was any work. I asked when I could come to work and he said, "Two weeks." Stalwart that I am, I've never gone anywhere else.

Q: What has kept you here for such a long time?

ADOPTABLE ANIMALS FROM THE SAN FRANCISCO A.S.P.C.A. TAKE CENTER RING IN THE GUMP'S CIRCUS WINDOWS.

A great love affair with the store. I grew up at the end of the depression. The family didn't really have anything. Any time my mother would get a gift from Gump's, for a birthday or Christmas, or something like that, no matter what it was, it meant more to her than anything else. Gump's was sort of instilled in me when I was very, very young. I can remember coming downtown with her and visiting the store. She loved the store, so I grew up loving the store.

Q: When you were a younger man, you wanted to be an architect. In your work you are an architect—of the windows.
Yes. I designed a house for a family friend when I was sixteen and it was built according to my plans. It is important to understand construction and I don't design anything unless I can understand how it can be built.

Q: How do you come up with your ideas for displays?
I don't know exactly. Oddly, the best ideas I have ever had happen when I am shaving. I work from the merchandise and usually it will suggest something to me, whether it will be color or design.

Q: What are some of your secrets for success?
I like to work a lot with "negative space." The position of the object is in relationship to the cube of the window itself, and the Asian concept of using odd-numbered objects, I think, also makes more interesting visuals.

Q: Are you a perfectionist?
I like to be. Detail is very important to me; I notice everything.

Q: Do you think that the general public has an inherent appreciation of all the work that goes into window designs?
Most people don't take the time to really look, but when they do, I think they "get" it. Oddly enough, the more minutely detailed a window you have, the more chance you have of stopping people to look. You can make people focus and see.

Q: What do you think the function of the windows is?
To sell merchandise. One of the best windows I ever designed was one of the quickest things I ever did. We ran out of

Once again, Ruffie started off to spend some quiet time in the art gallery. Soon he chose the perfect spot and climbed up on a bench. It was right smack in front of a Pablo Picasso (Pick-aw-so) etching, a Georges Braque (Brawk) lithograph, a David Hockney watercolor, and a Richard Diebenkorn graphic. Quite extraordinary for a store. This looked more like a museum, Ruffie thought.

It wasn't long before he was imagining himself visiting all the faraway art galleries he had only heard about. The Louvre (Loov-ruh), Jeu de Paume (Joo-duh-Poam), Musée d'Orsay (Moo-zay door-say), in Paris, France; the Prado (Praw-doh) in Madrid, Spain; the Tate (Tayt) and National Galleries in London, England. Ruffie was especially lucky because his former owner had been an art teacher and pets always learn so much from their families.

With a start, Ruffie realized he had been sitting and staring for a long while. "That's not fair," he thought to himself. "The time went by much too fast!"

23

merchandise in a window, since a customer bought what was in it. I grabbed a sheet of black cardboard and I stapled it up to the back wall so it curved down and I ran upstairs and I took three crystal glasses, the three most expensive glasses we had. I put them on the black, put three lights on them and wrote in chalk, "$87.50 each." (This was some years ago.) I walked out in front of the store to see if everything looked all right and I thought, "Wow, this is great." It cost about a dollar and a half to do it, too.

Q: Do you ever consider the window displays as an art form instead of just window dressing?
I never really approach it as an art form, but it turns out that it becomes one. I know so many other people who are better at things, but if I have a vision, I am good at getting it produced. A lot of people can see this vision, but they don't know how to go about getting it done. I am probably the most practical display director who has ever been at Gump's.

Q: Of the three or four thousand windows you've done, do you have any favorites?
The Fabergé eggs were my favorite, and it was the only Christmas display that I totally designed myself. I have always admired the jeweler Fabergé and understood the hours and hours of work that went into his eggs. Also the windows with the black shelf, the red plate, and the plaster letters spelling "Red China"; that was high art to me.

Q: What was your most challenging project?
I would say the "Tribute to Italy" promotion. Since I am constantly trying to exceed myself and an entire store display was something that I hadn't done, I was determined that it would outdo anything I'd seen. The Italian courtyard that we built was really solid. Anything that the public can touch has got to be as close to real as possible. We put it all together in one weekend, and the results were really spectacular. I was standing with the Italian ambassador, who flew out from Washington for the event, and we were gazing at the displays when he said to me, "Ah, it makes me feel like home." It was a wonderful feeling.

Q: How would you characterize Gump's display style?
It's definitely a different image, embodying simplicity, purpose, and visual communication that is unlike anyone else's.

JANET LYNN ROSEMAN

ABOVE: *CHRISTMAS AT GUMP'S,* A BOOK BY MIMI MCALLISTER FOR CHILDREN (AND ADULTS), WAS INSPIRED BY THE HOLIDAY WINDOWS AT GUMP'S FEATURING ADOPTABLE AND COMPLETELY CHARMING PETS FROM THE ASPCA. THE STORY FOLLOWS SIX OF THE ANIMALS AS THEY FROLIC THROUGH THE STORE AND CELEBRATE THEIR OWN SPECIAL HOLIDAY. ILLUSTRATIONS BY MARION KEEN.

RIGHT: THE RARE ARTISTRY OF OLD WORLD TECHNIQUES ARE NEVER MORE APPARENT THAN IN THESE HAND-CAST BRONZE FIGURINES FROM VIENNA. THIS CITY HAS BEEN THE HOME OF THE FINEST BRONZE CASTING TECHNIQUES FOR OVER A CENTURY. SINCE THE 1890s, THE ART OF BRONZE CASTING HAS DEVELOPED AND FLOUR-ISHED AT THE HANDS OF LOCAL ARTISANS. THEY HAVE SUCCEEDED IN COPYING NATURE WHILE PRESERVING THE HUMAN AND ANIMAL KINGDOM WITH A TOUCH OF WHIMSY. THESE BRONZE MINIATURES ARE COLLECTED BY CONNOISSEURS WHO SEEK REMEMBRANCES OF OLD VIENNA.

PRICE IS NO OBJECT

The "smart set" has always shopped Gump's. Even though the store carries gift items in the six figures, these are not always the best loved by the devoted and well-heeled patrons. A notable California family has as the dining room table centerpiece a sterling silver pagoda from Tiffany. Inside the pagoda one might expect to see a rare treasure, but inside this piece lies a $20 glass holly-berry tree, a favorite of its owner. Children with $10 as well as grown-ups with $10,000 know they can find just the right thing. The "Seiji" vase, the store's single largest-selling item, costs $20.

THESE DEEPLY COLORED SMOOTH-AS-SATIN CRYSTAL FISH SWIMMING OFF THE PAGE WERE ORIGINALLY DESIGNED BY THE MASTER CRAFTSMAN RENE LALIQUE IN 1932. LALIQUE BEGAN HIS CAREER AS A GRAPHIC ARTIST AND LATER CREATED MAGNIFICENT PIECES OF GEMS AND JEWELS AS WELL AS EXTRAORDINARY GLASSWARE. HIS FORAY INTO GLASSWORKS HAPPENED ACCIDENTALLY AS HE SOUGHT NEW MATERIALS WITH WHICH TO WORK. HE EVENTUALLY DISCOVERED GLASS TO BE A MEDIUM WELL SUITED TO HIS DESIGNS AND IN WHICH HE EXCELLED. IN 1918, HE ESTABLISHED HIS OWN FACTORY TO PRODUCE EXQUISITE AND FINELY-DETAILED DECORATIVE PIECES RANGING FROM GLASS CAR MASCOTS TO BOWLS AND PLATES. IN HIS HANDS, EACH PIECE WAS TRULY ONE OF BEAUTY. LALIQUE'S LOVE AND APPRECIATION OF NATURE AND THE IMPACT OF HIS CHILDHOOD SUMMERS IN CHAMPAGNE HAD A PROFOUND EFFECT ON HIS WORK. FLOWERS AND WILDLIFE WERE SOURCES OF INSPIRATION, AND IMAGES OF THE NATURAL WORLD CHARACTERIZED THE VERY ESSENCE OF HIS ART. HE "BADE NATURE DISCLOSE ITS SECRETS. IT RESPONDED."

INSIDE THE STORE: THE GREAT SHOWS

In the early 1980s the San Francisco store underwent a significant renovation. It was time to announce to San Francisco that there was fresh excitement at Gump's, and this was done by launching a series of fall shows in the San Francisco store.

A TRIBUTE TO ITALY

The first, "A Tribute to Italy," opened in 1984 with a gala black tie reception hosted by the Italian ambassador to the United States, Rinaldo Petrignani. The entire first floor was transformed into a two-story Palladian villa with the Lion of Venice presiding atop a twenty-foot column in the center. The Gump's buyers introduced the work of Carlo Moretti, one of the finest contemporary glassmakers, and beautiful Venini glass and other pieces filled the room. The ceiling of an adjacent room was tented in Venetian silk, and Oriental carpets covered the tabletops in a display of Italian and Oriental goods reminiscent of Marco Polo's days. Buccellati, Ricci, and other fine Italian silversmiths sent spectacular pieces, and in the China Department, Gump's presented an entire new dinner service, Granduca, produced by Ginori at the request of the store. To complement this dinner service, Gump's arranged for the loan—the first ever granted by the Doccia Museum—of 130 pieces of the earliest porcelain pieces manufactured.

"FÊTE CHAMPÊTRE." THIS TRIBUTE TO A FABLED 18TH CENTURY GARDEN SAW THE MODEL ROOM TRANSFORMED INTO THE GROTTOLIKE ENTRANCE OF THE ANCIENT FOLIE. 1987.

Gump's also exhibited one of the greatest draws ever seen in the opera-conscious city of San Francisco—the Verdi collection from the museum at La Scala. From Verdi's ceremonial gold and diamond baton to his personal prized possessions, paintings, scores, and libretti, the exhibit was unprecedented outside Italy. In fact, this collection had never before been allowed on loan, and the permission of the Italian government was required in order for the collection to leave the country.

Countess Gozzi of Fortuny helped create a model room in the store. She was kind enough to share her remnant collection, including antique fabrics, with the Gump's buyers, and these fabrics were used to make clothing for hand-made Italian dolls, eyeglass case covers, and jewelry boxes.

The excitement generated by the exhibition was enormous: The *San Francisco Examiner*'s *Sunday* section ran a full-color section on the Verdi Collection, *Opera Magazine* carried a full story on it as well, and *Connoisseur* featured an article about the Granduca porcelain. The two-week event was extended to a third week, and more than a quarter of a million visitors saw "A Tribute to Italy."

BRITISH STYLE

Once the precedent was begun, Gump's sponsored other shows. In 1985, "British Style" featured great white gazebos as display pieces, encountered once one passed through a special tea and scent shop entrance. Each of the store's departments created special merchandise, but the highlight of the show was the involvement of the Churchill family. Lord Charles Spencer-Churchill accompanied his wife Jane to Gump's and helped host the opening. Jane Churchill had designed a line of fabrics and wallcoverings, and Gump's recreated her London shop, bringing her work to America for the first time. At the same time, a limited edition reprint of Winston Churchill's *Painting as a Pastime* was commissioned by Gump's with an introduction by the statesman's grandson. The younger Churchill attended a mobbed booksigning where the limited edition completely sold out.

The real draw of the show, however, was an exhibition of the oil paintings of Sir Winston Churchill. The only prior American showings of his work on this scale had been at the Metropolitan Museum of Art in New York and the Smithsonian Institution in Washington, D. C. The twenty-two paintings exhibited were lent by private individuals and institutions in a wonderful spirit of cooperation. From the former prime minister the Rt. Hon. Edward Heath to Cambridge University to Her Grace, Lavinia, Duchess of Norfolk and many others, the response was generous and willing. Several hundred thousand people stood in line to view the paintings.

PORTS OF CALL

For Gump's 125th anniversary celebration in 1986, the store designed vignettes of its past and hosted an opening benefit evening for the Edgewood Children's Center. There were three extraordinary exhibits in the show. The first was a model room in tribute to Eleanor Forbes, Gump's legendary designer, prepared by John and Elinor McGuire, for whom Eleanor had designed a first line of wicker furniture. Searching for a second special exhibit, William Goulet, the store's vice president in charge of these special events, visited with Diana Vreeland, who suggested "look to your roots—show something Chinese such as the emperor's clothes." Her inspiration led to the rich exhibit "The Robes of the Emperor, His Imperial and Princely Families." In looking to its roots, the store also mounted a special art show titled "Recollections: 125 Years of California Artists at Gump's," featuring the works of artists who had exhibited at the store. All works were for sale and the show was a sellout, proving to be a watershed exhibit for older California artists, and the market for their works has risen enormously.

FÊTE CHAMPETRE, FABLED LANDS, AND PLACES IN THE SUN

A 1987 show was a French celebration of an antique fantasy garden under current restoration. Parts of the garden were recreated inside the store with thousands of fresh flowers on tables, entryways, and special shops. In 1988 Gump's paid tribute to the fabled lands of literature and filled the windows with giant books illustrating far-off lands. On the main floor was a huge silver Corinthian column topped with a silver camel, surrounded with golden palm leaves and supporting an enormous Lalique-style bowl overflowing with flowers. In the Art Gallery an exhibit of 19th Century luminist visions of America ranged from the Hudson River School to California artist Maynard Dixon. The following year, 1989, the Art Gallery again stole the thunder of the annual show with "Artists of the Americas," one of the first Hispanic art shows presented by a mainstream contemporary art gallery in America. "Places in the Sun" also captured the public's fancy, when Gump's flooded its storefront windows and had them filled with live exotic fish from the Steinhardt Aquarium.

Through the years the shows have demonstrated Gump's' commitment to finding and presenting, in a most elegant and exciting fashion, the very finest of the world's goods.

WILLIAM GOULET

LEFT: "FABLED LANDS." THE MAIN FLOOR HOUSED A TWO-STORY CAMEL IN FLORAL, GOLD, AND SILVER TRAPPINGS. 1988.

RIGHT: BACCARAT. THE "CRYSTAL OF KINGS" HAS EARNED ITS MORE THAN TWO-CENTURY-OLD REPUTATION THROUGH ITS SUPERB DESIGN, EXQUISITE CLARITY, AND FAULTLESS QUALITY. FOUNDED IN FRANCE IN 1764, BY WRIT OF LOUIS XV, THE CRISTALLERIES DE BACCARAT ARE NOTED FOR A COMMITMENT TO EXCELLENCE. THE WORKMANSHIP AND SIGNATURE DESIGNS HAVE BEEN REVERED BY COLLECTORS INTERNATIONALLY...AND LITTLE WONDER. MANY OF THE BACCARAT CRAFTSMEN HOLD THE TITLE "MEILLEUR OUVRIER DE FRANCE," AN HONOR BESTOWED UPON THEM BY THE PRESIDENT OF FRANCE IN RECOGNITION OF THE NATION'S SKILLED ARTISANS.

One of Gump's memorable shows was "A Tribute to Italy" in 1984. No expense was spared in order to present the finest Italian objets d'art. To acquire and assemble a collection of regional artisans' work, Gump's executives travelled throughout the country in search of cottage industries, small shops, and individual craftsmen. They brought back marvelous treasures: fantastic feathered carnival and commedia dell' arte masks; handmade peasant dolls; boxes of lapis-lazuli and malachite. They borrowed Verdi artifacts from the La Scala Museum that had never been seen outside Italy. A bronze bust of Verdi made in 1872 was a favorite of an anonymous San Franciscan who returned day after day during the exhibit to place a single rose on its pedestal. Gump's has presented numerous special exhibits and promotions with equal panache.

GUMP'S ADVERTISING: DURING THE 1980S, GUMP'S' RETAIL ADVERTISING, PARTICULARLY FOR ITS FINE CHINA, CRYSTAL, AND SILVER, GAINED NATIONAL ATTENTION THROUGH *TOWN & COUNTRY*, *CONNOISSEUR*, *GOURMET*, *ARCHITECTURAL DIGEST*, AND *ELLE DECOR*.

RIGHT: "DUTCH WOMAN HOLDING A GLASS AND
ADMIRING AN INFANT." 1860. WOOD BLOCK
PRINT.

OPPOSITE: "FOREIGNERS WATCHING LION
DANCERS." 1861. WOOD BLOCK PRINT.

阿蘭陀婦人

嬰䑾

愛兒童

之圖

WEST MEETS EAST
JAPANESE PRINTS PORTRAY THE FIRST YEARS OF TRADE WITH THE WEST

Richard B. Gump, former Asian Art Commissioner and Honorary Commissioner since 1976, donated to the Asian Art Museum an important group of Nagasaki and Yokohama prints from the second half of the 19th Century. The museum received these works with considerable delight, as they added an entirely new dimension to its holdings. Immediately planned was a special exhibition of these prints, and Mr. Gump responded with his usual generosity by assuming the sponsorship of both the exhibition and its catalogue, a unique gesture in the annals of the museum.

The Richard Gump Collection spans the forty years or so that it took Japan to become a major world power; 1860 marked the official opening of the country to foreign trade, since on May 17 of that year the first Japanese embassy to Washington ratified a commercial treaty that had been sought by the United States as early as 1851. The year 1894 saw the outbreak of the Sino-Japanese War, which led to the Japanese domination of Korea. However, the bulk of the prints correspond to the first twelve years of this revolutionary era, when Westerners in Yokohama and things Western were captured *de visu* by the startled eyes of unprepared Japanese artists. These prints also deal almost exclusively with the two ports open to foreign trade, Nagasaki and Yokohama—with a few exceptions.

Nagasaki had been opened to foreign ships and traders as early as 1570, but in 1639 all foreigners were expelled with the exception of the Chinese and the Dutch, the latter being confined to the man-made islet of Deshima. Thus, the relatively massive appearance in the late 1860s of other nationals, such as the Russians, must have created considerable interest.

The impact on Yokohama was staggering. In 1859 the town was just a small fishing village. Thirty years later it counted a population of over one hundred thousand. The craze for Yokohama prints was short-lived. Most of them were produced between 1861 and 1864, as reflected by the present collection. This phenomenon is generally attributed to the serious inflation that hit the inhabitants of this booming city in the mid 1860s.

These prints can be regarded as an offshoot of the ukiyo-e school. In fact, the Utagawa print masters who spurred the new movement in Nagasaki and Yokohama traced the roots of their school to the celebrated Utagawa Toyoharu of Edo (1735-1814). Yet Nagasaki and Yokohama prints differ from their predecessors in inspiration, style, and usage.

One of the main themes consists of the portrayal of the foreigners themselves. Americans, Chinese, Dutch, English, French, and Russians, these exotic people are depicted in what was then regarded as typical attitudes. Their stature and facial features are exaggerated to the point where they look like benevolent giants, especially when shown side by side with Japanese people. Whether or not the caricatural touch was entirely intentional remains open to question, but there is no doubt that these "portraits" are a far cry from the idealized renderings of the ukiyo-e school. In their avid curiosity, the printmakers and their clientele longed for more than could actually be seen in the harbors and streets of Nagasaki and Yokohama. They wanted to know how foreigners lived in their own countries, hence some rather imaginative renderings of distant cities.

In general, these prints reveal a certain crudeness in approach, which was due to the necessity of producing them as cheaply as possible. The images were made as souvenirs for the masses and produced accordingly. The materials used, including the paper, were not made to last, and it is a marvel that quite a few prints have survived this long. Conversely, the traditional division of labor was respected and guaranteed a certain level of quality, at least for Yokohama prints that were made in Edo, and the names of the print masters and of the publishers together with the dates of manufacture are faithfully recorded.

In brief, this group of prints constitutes a most valuable source of information on one of the most exciting and portentous moments of the history of Japan.

RENÉ-YVON LEFEBVRE D'ARGENCE, Director
YOSHIKO KAKUDO, Curator of Japanese Art
The Asian Art Museum of San Francisco

Reprinted with permission.

EXPECT THE UNEXPECTED

Shoppers at Gump's expect to see beautiful merchandise attractively displayed, that is a given. But many come just to see the window displays or smell the fresh flower arrangements, which are ever changing. Long-time patrons and tourists alike know that they can handle pieces from the largest collection of Baccarat and Steuben crystal in this museumlike setting, since touching is not discouraged. Gump's unique presentation has made it a "must-see" and a "must-do" on San Francisco's list of sights and attractions.

THE REGAL APPEARANCE OF THE BACCARAT, LALIQUE, AND STEUBEN ROOMS ARE MUSEUMLIKE IN PRESENTATION AND DAZZLING TO THE EYE. GUMP'S OFFERS THE LARGEST COLLECTION OF BACCARAT IN THE UNITED STATES, EXCEPT FOR BACCARAT'S OWN SHOWROOM.

Gump's has received letters over the years, and although some customers become confused or careless in identifying the store's name, somehow the mail always gets through. One letter was delivered, appropriately enough, to:
Gump's
250 POSH Street
San Francisco
California

Where else but at Gump's would you find Winston Churchill's oil paintings or the largest Buddha of its kind outside a museum towering above Oriental treasures? Would another retailer recreate an Italian villa sufficiently beautiful and perfect in form and presentation that the Italian ambassador would comment it was so authentic it felt like home? What other store windows would feature ASPCA-facilitated adoptable puppies and kittens as a Christmas crowd-pleaser and simultaneous fund-raiser? Nowhere else, and no one else can do what Gump's does so well. Loyal shoppers and staff alike have learned to expect the unexpected. It's a stimulating, creative, original way to run a modern emporium with a vast array of personal, ornamental, collectible, and museum-quality merchandise. *Gump's!*

BIBLIOGRAPHY

Books

Anscombe, Isabelle. *A Woman's Touch: Women in Design from 1860 to the Present Day* (New York: Viking, 1984).

Beebe, Lucius. *The Big Spenders* (New York: Doubleday and Company, 1966).

Birmingham, Stephen. *The Right People: A Portrait of the American Social Establishment* (Boston: Little, Brown and Company, 1960).

Buck, Pearl S. *My Several Worlds: A Personal Record* (New York: Day and Company, 1954).

DeWolfe, Elsie. *The House in Good Taste* (New York: Century and Company, 1913.)

Duncan, Alistair. *Art Deco* (London: Thames and Hudson, 1988).

Gump, Richard. *Good Taste Costs No More* (New York: Doubleday and Company, 1951.)

_____. *Jade: Stone of Heaven* (New York: Doubleday and Company, 1962).

Gump, Robert. *Chinese Rugs* (self-published, San Francisco, c. 1925).

_____. *You are the Rose, You are the Rock: An Eastern Logic* (Philadelphia: Dorrance and Company, 1967).

Henri, Robert. *The Art Spirit* (New York: HarperCollins/Lippincott, 1923).

1904-1905 San Francisco: Her Great Manufacturing, Commercial and Financial Institutions are Famed the World Over (San Francisco: The Pacific Art Company, 1904).

Post, Emily. *By Motor to the Golden Gate* (New York: Appleton & Company, 1916).

Riess, Suzanne B. *Richard Gump: Composer, Artist, and President of Gump's San Francisco*. An interview published by the Regional Oral History Office of the Bancroft Library, the Regents of the University of California (1989).

Wigman, Mary. *The Creative Process* (New York: New American Library, 1952).

Wilson, Carol Green. *Gump's Treasure Trade: A Story of San Francisco* (New York: HarperCollins/T. Y. Crowell Company, 1949).

Articles

Behbehani, Mandy. "Behind the Swank Curtain," *Image* magazine, *San Francisco Sunday Chronicle and Examiner,* September 25, 1986.

d'Argence, Rene-Yvon Lefebvre, and Yoshiko Kakudo. "West Meets East: Japanese Prints Portray the First Years of Trade from the West," Asian Art Museum, San Francisco, 1981.

Green, Lois Wagner. "Eleanor Forbes: Full of Functional Gumption," *San Francisco Sunday Chronicle and Examiner,* January 22, 1948.

Gump, A. L., with Frank J. Taylor. "From Saloon to Salon," *The Saturday Evening Post*, June 20, 1936.

Mannel, Elise. "Eleanor Forbes: Design Consultant," *San Francisco Chronicle,* September 5, 1948.

Perry, Kris. "Gump's: From Saloon to Nob Hill Society," *Nob Hill Gazette,* March 1982.

Schlesinger, Ellen. "What Metal Miracle Have the Grags Wrought?," *The Sacramento Bee,* September 6, 1984.